radical hot rods

GRAFFITI

Published in 2002 by
Graffiti Publications Pty Ltd
69 Forest Street, Castlemaine, Victoria, Australia
Phone International: 61 3 5472 3653
Fax International: 61 3 5472 3805
Email: graffiti@netcon.net.au
Website: www.graffitipub.com.au

Copyright 2002 by Larry O'Toole
Publisher: Larry O'Toole
Design: Michael deWolfe
Production: Mary-Anna Brennand

Cover Photos: Rod Hadfield's incredible 1919 Model T coupe is hand built and powered by a twin blown Boss 429 Ford engine.
The fad style T coupe is Australia's most radical street rod that was built over a 26 year period.

Film Production: Sharpscan, West Melbourne, Victoria Australia
Printing: Centre State Printers, Maryborough, Victoria Australia.

The information in this book is true and complete to the best of our knowledge. All recommendations are made without any guarantee
on the part of the author or publisher, who also disclaim any liability incurred in connection with the use of this data or specific details.
Some photographs in this publication have been digitally enhanced.

Graffiti Publications books are also available at discounts in bulk quantity for industrial or sales promotional use.
For details contact Graffiti Publications PH. 61 3 5472 3653

Printed and bound in Australia.

ISBN 0 949398 74 8

The Lo-Life High school bus is Jerry Bowes'
contribution to the world of Radical Hot Rods,
shown here at the NSRA Street Rod Nationals.

contents

introduction
Larry O'Toole

Showcased in this publication is a selection of the most outrageous hot rods in the world. All the color and spectacle of the top end of hot rodding comes together in this full color book. Monstrous blown engines, huge wheels and tires, extreme styling and exotic, advanced engineering are the ingredients that combine together to become the radical hot rods of the modern era. These are the hot rods that stop you in your tracks, not necessarily practical, but certainly spectacular. Dozens of the best examples in the world are shown in full color mini-features throughout this book.

Most hot rodders are content to stay within what we might call the traditional, conservative parameters of hot rodding but as in all walks of life there are those who like to push the boundaries of conventional style to the limits. These are the hot rodders who are not content to have another tidy street rod. Their hot rods are of the type that demand attention, if not through brute "in-your-face" demonstrations of enormous horsepower potential in the engine bay, then definitely through extremes of styling, or the application of advanced engineering concepts. These are the blatant show cars, the drag strip phantoms and the clever projects that make us all stop and take another look.

Just as the mass production automotive manufacturers build extreme design concept cars to test public reaction, so the radical hot rods of our hobby test our own reactions. And as with the factory concept cars, many elements of these leading edge vehicles eventually filter down to the masses, often in somewhat more conservative fashion, but nevertheless exerting their influence on hot rodders everywhere.

This book is a tribute to those hot rodders who think outside the square, who challenge our ideas of the practical and who dare to be different in an increasingly sterile world.

Larry O'Toole

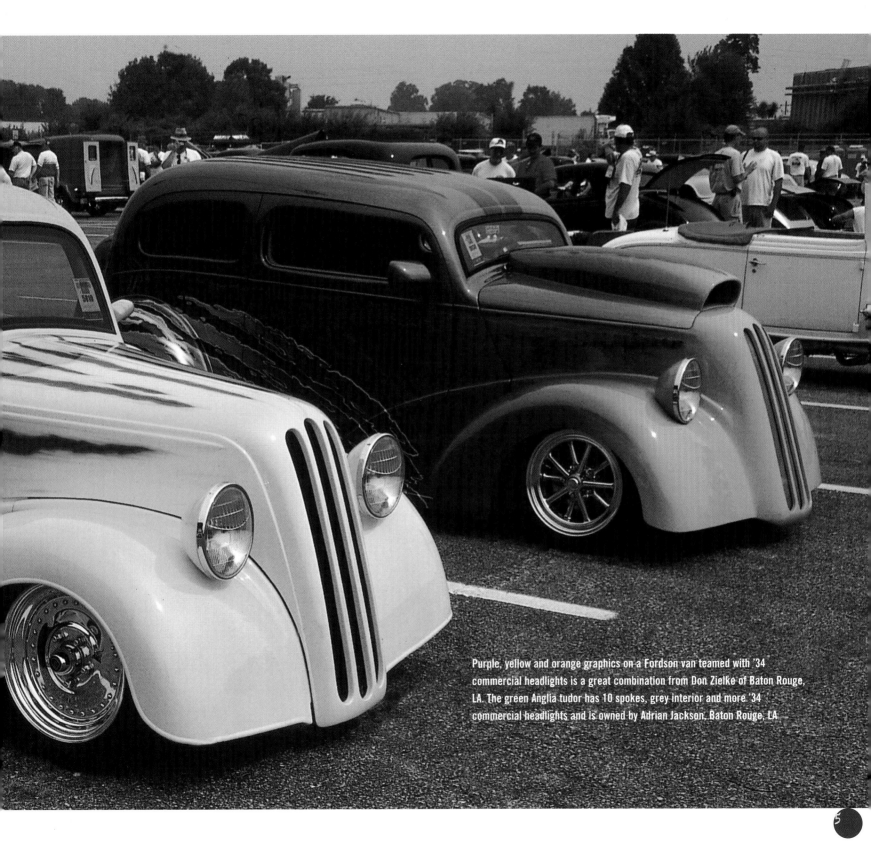

Purple, yellow and orange graphics on a Fordson van teamed with '34 commercial headlights is a great combination from Don Zielke of Baton Rouge, LA. The green Anglia tudor has 10 spokes, grey interior and more. '34 commercial headlights and is owned by Adrian Jackson, Baton Rouge, LA

John Coute
1932 Ford Roadster
Highland, CA USA

Halibrand wheels are always right at home on a traditional Deuce hiboy and a blown small block Chevy is fairly common too, but this one owned by John Coute takes on a much more radical persona thanks to those zoomy exhaust cutouts that can be operated on the move. You really notice when they slide open as the roadster passes by! Once you overcome the initial reaction you might also see the cream leather interior and Stewart Warner gauges along with the polished steering column and tri-spoke wheel. Adding to the individual radical design is a clever half roll-cage blended into the interior. Protecting that interior from the elements, when necessary, is a solid lift-off top. A Hilborn scoop tops the engine package in typical menacing fashion. Tires are Firestone P275/60 R17 rears and Toyo P185/60 R14 on the front.

C. Mark Race
1936 Ford Roadster
Fort Dodge, IA USA

Believe it or not this '36 Ford roadster is an all-steel body that was found in a barn and had been last titled in 1964. In its new street rod form the body has been shaved, the fenders have been widened $1\frac{1}{2}$ inches at the rear and the fronts have been altered to allow the suicide doors to open without hitting. Mercedes E320 lights are blended into the fenders and the grille was custom made from stainless steel by Grille Art and then chromed for even brighter effect. Covering the engine bay is a three piece hood made from stock parts and mounted on hinges set into the firewall to facilitate opening alligator style.

The engine is a 383 stroker small block Chevy by Barrett Engines that pumps out 450hp and 480lbs/ft of torque. It is backed up with a Turbo 700R4 from Hawaii Racing in California.

Under the rear of the chassis is an eight inch Ford rear end with 3.55:1 gears and it is held in place by a four-bar with Air-Ride suspension. The roadster sits on a custom Fatman Chassis made from 2x4 tube. Braking is handled by Wilwood Blue Ice eleven inch discs, while the wheels are Boyd Coddington 20x10$\frac{1}{2}$ inch and 17x7 inch with Michelin Z rated tires.

The interior is trimmed in beige leather by Jim McFarlane using Intrepid seats and incorporating Phipps handles in the door trims. VDO gauges fill the dash, an Ididit column with Billet Specialties wheel lets the driver control directions and a Lokar shifter brings the driveline into play. Entertainment is provided by an Eclipse stereo with six-disc changer.

Bobby Alloway
1933 Trackstar
Knoxville, TN USA

Track nose hot rods were rarely as sleek as this one built by hot rod master craftsman Bobby Alloway. That's because the body is a Speed Star item that Bobby had designed in 2000. It used to have a conventional '33 grille at the front but it was changed over to a track nose for a totally new look that Bobby calls a Trackstar.

The Trackstar has a $119\frac{1}{2}$ inch wheelbase with a five-inch drop Super Bell front axle, quarter elliptic springs and Functional Freight brake drums from So-Cal. In the rear there's a Winters Straight 2 quick change held in place by a Pete and Jake four-bar. Wheels are ET3 with Halibrand knockoffs, 16x10 on the rear with Michelin 275/70 tires while the skinny fronts have 135/75/15 tires.

Power comes from a 454 that has been bored .030" over resulting in 462 cubic inches, fed by a single Holley 850 double pumper carburetor. Transmission is a Turbo 350 and cooling is trusted to a Steve Long radiator from Indianapolis, Indiana.

The body retains the original Speedstar cabriolet back half and is painted in Dupont black basecoat/clearcoat. Commercial '33 Ford headlights and '39 Chevrolet taillights

are the only interruptions to that super smooth body style on the outside. Inside the talented Paul Atkins out of Comer, Alabama attended to the interior trim in black leather. Ididit supplied the steering column that is topped with a Pete and Jake steering wheel and kept company by a Lokar shifter. Moon gauges are fitted to a Carriage Works gauge panel to complete the interior fittings.

Gary Smith is one of those consummate hot rodders who can afford to own the ultimate, not once, but twice over. The black with flames Willys coupe he commissioned from Clayton Custom Cars, out of Benson, North Carolina who primarily just build Willys. They started with a rectangular seamless tube chassis, the outside rails of which are 2x3 and 2x4 inch, while all the tubes in between, front to rear, are $1\frac{1}{2}$ inch mandrel bent round tubing.

This particular car has a New Generation 502 from GM which has aluminum heads. It was bored .030" to make sure everything was clean and round and everything fitted correctly. A bigger cam went in, together with a little head work, and then the whole lot was put back together. On top went a BDS 8.7:1 blower that has been indexed so it all runs correctly and then topped with two tricked-out Barry Grant 750 carbs. Just for good measure it has a 500hp nitrous system as well.

A 3000 rpm stall speed converter feeds on to a Turbo 400 transmission, beefed up to take the

increased horsepower. A coupe with this much power also needs to stop well so it was equipped with four-wheel disc brakes and a 10 inch disc brake on the third member. That third member is a hand fabricated nine inch sheet metal rear end fitted with 35 spline axles. A separate master cylinder housed under the console is used to hydraulically operate the emergency brake so when you pull the arm it actually quirts brake fluid right into the cylinder at 1900 psi. This car has 1126 horsepower (dynoed) and when you pull the emergency brake up three notches, put it in first gear and nail it, the motor will die; the emergency brake will not let the tires spin. This is a great safety factor as it means if you lose the brakes driving down the road, you can stop the car with the emergency brake.

The air-conditioning condenser is mounted behind the third member on the chassis and it has a fan that pulls 3150 cfm. No matter what the temperature is in the radiator, turning the air-conditioner on does not affect it at all. Steve Long of Custom Radiators combined with Frank Mandari of Clayton Custom Cars to make the radiator and the one in this car has never seen 190°F even with an 1126 horsepower engine and with the air-conditioning on!

The special wheels were actually designed to suit this car. With most Pro Street cars you can't get the back wheel and tire out unless you get the car way up in the air and drop the rear end. The tires were selected first, they are BF Goodrich 345/55/17s originally made for the front of a five-yard cement truck, but there was no readily available wheel that would fit in the Willys wheel well with the right offsets. Budnik were commissioned to make the rear wheels for the car. They are 17 inch diameter with 13 inch width, but with only a two inch backspace. That makes the wheel 11 inches deep, which is as deep as any Pro Street wheel, it just doesn't have a lot of it on the inside. As a result the coupe can run radial tires, drive in the rain, stop well, get good bite and be driven anytime, anywhere without any wobble. The lug nuts can be taken off and the wheel removed by just raising the coupe like a normal car. The wheel and tire will come right off because it only has two inches of backspace. The front wheels are 17x7 inch with 4.125 inch backspacing with a 215/40/17 tire, so there is about 8½ inches of tire on the front and about 14 inches on the back. Gary claims the car really does handle like it should.

Front suspension is independent Heidts with stainless steel top and bottom pivoting arms. The Aldan gas shockers have five position settings so you can change the ride from a nice ride if you are going on a trip to a hard ride if you're going racing. Gary describes it as a fun car to drive around corners. The exhaust uses Sanderson headers and a three inch stainless tube from the header collector all the way under the back with custom made mufflers that are solid stainless inside and out and guaranteed for life. Each muffler has a different internal mechanism, so instead of just being loud it is tuned, giving the car a real nice sound.

The interior is all trimmed in a light beige buckskin leather with a trick console that was formed to fit the car. It has air-conditioning, defrost/air/heat, and all the amenities a normal car should feature, such as power windows and remote keyless power door locks. Windshield wipers are mounted below the windshield where most Willys have no wipers at all, or they are mounted above the windshield.

Gary Smith
1941 Willys Coupe
Sydney, OH USA

The yellow Willys coupe was also commissioned by Gary Smith from Clayton Custom Cars. Gary had seen a few cars around the country with Hemis in them and decided that if he was going to have a really bad Willys, it had to have a Hemi in it. This one started with a 1941 Willys body and the same tube chassis as the black car, with a few more strengthening bars in it. It has a sway bar in the rear, as it was felt that with 2000 plus horsepower on pump gas it would need every attention to detail. Apart from the front sway bar, it has 11-inch discs on the back while the front was treated to new 2850 psi clamping pressure calipers that really seem to work better. This particular car uses a lot of carbon fibre, featured on the trunk wall, floor mats, extended dash bottom and custom built door panels.

All the KB Hemi blocks were styled on the 426 Hemis, but Kenneth Black, who now owns Keith Black Racing since his father passed away, made this block for 676 cubic inches and it's based on a Top Fuel block. He actually cast some water jackets into it for this application so that it does have water running through it. The block is an eight cross-bolted main block with four bolts on the inside of the block and four bolts outside the block on each main webbing. It has a Top Fuel crank, rods, pistons and all the big, big boy stuff. The heads are Indy cylinder heads with 16 spark plugs – two per cylinder. A special water pump by Meziere was made specifically for this car and it actually moves four times the amount of water of the more common water pumps. A diverter plate was made for this motor so the water comes out of the radiator into the water pump, then it gets diverted to the heads first, the reverse of most systems. It works well as this car has never been over 175°F. Right now the engine is detuned, making 11 pounds of boost, but it still makes 2016 horsepower on the dyno, on pump gas! This motor has the potential for almost 6000 horsepower if run with nitro-methane in it and the boost pumped up. It has a 10-71 BDS blower and two injection systems. It has a 16 hard line nozzle system on top of the blower that makes the motor run from idle. When the computer reads its sensors and says the revs are at top end and leaning out, it opens one more injector nozzle on each side of the motor that squirts fuel below the blower. There's another 16 hard-lines under the blower that feeds the blower more fuel to prevent lean out and burnt pistons. Then it has a 1500 hp nitrous kit on top of the blower if you want some more horsepower.

The radiator is very large on this particular car, 37 inches wide and developed especially for this application. The radiator actually goes out into the fender-wells where there's a five-inch pocket in each fender well.

For fitting, the radiator slides up from the bottom. With all this radiator there is no cooling problem even though the coupe has Vintage Air air-conditioning, that's because it has the condenser and fans behind the third member where it doesn't affect the running temperature of the car.

Transmission is a reverse manual valve body equipped Turbo 400 with a trans-brake, all set for drag racing if Gary wants to go do the drag race thing after the newness gets rubbed off the car. An aluminum adaptor plate was used to bolt the transmission to the Hemi. Zoomy headers were built for the car with 2½ inch primary tubes. Each individual tube has a DOT approved muffler fitted inside. Budnik wheels are again one-off manufacture. These are the first Gasser wheels made by Budnik and they made a carbon-fiber Gasser steering wheel to match the big five-inch carbon fiber monster gauges from Auto Meter. The nitrous bottles are mounted in the trunk and are all chromed.

The rear end features a sheet-metal housing all tricked out with a Strange spool, and 35 spline axles. The really unusual flames on both cars use Harlequin PPG paint but the yellow car has a really wild set of flames that are unique to this car. The yellow is a custom color used on only two cars in the world. NAPA won't tell Gary what the color is, he just got three gallons of paint for $US2700.00. Apparently it is a mixture of brands of paint supposedly by Martin Senior. Gary isn't able to confirm that information but says there are five pints of different pearls added per gallon. On the can it simply says; Yellow – Custom Mix. Taillights are flush while the third brake light is housed in the billet license plate frame.

Interior trim is leather, the Color of Spice, which is rather like a pumpkin color over custom seats by Cerullo, out of California. This coupe has a chrome moly cage in it along with full shoulder harnesses and belts. It has all the equipment required for safety. The console is carbon fiber, there's a mural on the dash that has the black car being sickled by the grim reaper and it has Bob Ida's orange Willys flipped upside down. It also has the Ridler award winning yellow speedstar car being torn up and it has Fred Burrows' green GMC truck (featured elsewhere in this book) also in the grips of the grim reaper.

Jim Fountain
1928 Model A Tudor,
Greenwood, IN USA

The basis of Jim Fountain's Vicky style Model A is a steel '29 tudor body on a '32 Ford frame that is welded to the body. Scott Graham of Generations Custom Auto and Collision helped with the project that saw the rear section of the body laid forward to give the "Vicky" styling to the car. The doors, which operate in suicide fashion have been lengthened four inches. The roof has been filled and chopped five inches before it was bathed in Dupont Orange tinter. Model A headlights are mounted to the sides of the grille shell to give an uncluttered appearance to the front view. The sunvisor has been shortened $1\frac{1}{2}$ inches while the hood is a custom made three piece unit that has the side panels punched full of hot rod style louvers.

Coil-over suspension is used front and rear with the front done in suicide style and located by a home-made four-bar system. A Vega steering box directs the course the Model A will take while the rear end has an eight inch third member and is also located by a home-made four bar. American Racing wheels are15x10 on the rear and 15x4 on the front with Goodrich 285/15 and 135/15 tires.

Drive train is all small block Chevy with a 350 engine coupled to a Turbo 350 transmission. Cooling is provided by a Walker radiator and a Mooneyes air cleaner keeps the intake free of debris. Inside there is a '40 Ford dash, a steering wheel by Pete and Jake mounted on a home-made column and beige leather is used over Mercury Capri bucket seats and the rest of the interior. The floor mounted shifter is by Gennie, tinted glass keeps the hot summer sun at bay and the windshield has been made to glue in place as on late model vehicles. Hidden clips hold the custom door trims in place.

Tucci Engineering were engaged to carry out the majority of the work on this most radical of trucks. They started with a mandrel bent Art Morrison 2x4 inch chassis that dumps the cab close to the ground and suspended it with Canover Air Ride equipment at the front and rear. The nine inch Ford rear end is held in place with a Morrison four link and equipped with Coleman disc rotors and Wilwood calipers. The front end features custom control arms by Tucci with Mustang II spindles and the same brake combination as used at the rear.

Powerplant is an injected 406 cubic inch small block Chevy put together by Boyd's motor Works of Mayfield, NY. It wears Brodix heads that are fed by an Accel fuel injection system with Throttle Engineering throttle bodies. The exhaust system is three inch diameter polished stainless steel.

A Lokar shifter is used to bring a Turbo 700R4 transmission into play and it has a GM lock-up 3,000 rpm stall speed converter plus Valley transmission shift kit fitted.

The GMC body is barely recognisable, it has been modified so heavily from the original by Garry Brown and Dave Tucci. Garry chopped the top six inches but left the rear window stock height and added a '54 Pontiac grille at the

rear through which the exhaust exits. Bullet taillights from a '57 Cadillac also adorn the rear end. Doug Moot and Bruce Crossway from State Bridge Collision were responsible for the rest of the body preparation prior to Doug spraying the House of Kolor Organic Green paint. The wildly reworked pickup bed is topped with a one-piece tilting cover made from aluminum, the headlights are from a Prowler and the grille was another custom made item by Tucci Engineering.

Wheels are 17 inch and 20 inch Colorado Custom items fitted with 225/45Rx17 Goodyear tires at the front and 295/40Rx20 Goodyears at the rear. Jerry and Sue Chambers from Jerry's Custom Upholstery trimmed the interior in bone leather over Tea's Design seats with a chromed tilt steering column from Ididit, topped by a Colorado Custom steering wheel. White face Pro Comp gauges live in a Prowler dash insert housed in a custom made dashboard while the Wireworks were responsible for the wiring in the pickup.

Terry Cook really set the rodding scene buzzing with the debut of his radical '39 Lincoln Zephyr coupe. Voluptuous is the only way to describe the extensively massaged body. It received an eight inch top chop, a '41 Zephyr nose graft and the doors now operate in suicide fashion. The hood was stretched one inch and now leads the viewer's eye to a Honda Accord windshield. The front fenders have been raised and fitted with '39 Ford headlight lenses while the rears have been extended six inches, adding to that swoopy styling. Only House of Kolor Passion Pearl would be right for this body and it is highlighted at the rear with a narrowed '54 Kaiser bumper.

The body has been channeled over a '78 Chevy wagon chassis that's been Zeed in the cowl area and stretched to match the Lincoln wheelbase. Hydraulic suspension means it can be dropped on the ground when parked and raised for driving. Power comes from a '74 Chevy 350 engine coupled to a Turbo 350 transmission and cooled by a Walker radiator, originally meant for a '40-'48 Plymouth. Normally the wheels are 14 inch steelies with Coker P205/75Rx14 tires and rippled Moon discs but Terry also has a 17 inch chromed Niche Bahn spare wheel that he sometimes fits to one side at the front, giving the car a different style when viewed from one side compared to the other.

Inside there is a '39 Zephyr dash that was modified by Ram's Rod Shop, who were responsible for all the bodywork. The stock Zephyr gauges are retained but converted to 12 volt operation and the passengers recline on a Cadillac six-way power operated split bench seat. Entertainment is provided by a Pioneer sound system and comfort is enhanced by Vintage Air air conditioning. Bobby Sapp was called in to trim the interior in simple black and white leather and naugahyde and a Ron Francis kit was used to wire the coupe. There is even a purple neon underneath the car for eerie night driving effects.

There was always one dream car that Rod Hadfield wanted to create, a Model T coupe with a twin blown engine. In October 1971, Rod parted with $900 for the origins of a Model T project. He set about building a Fad style tube chassis and mounting the '26 T coupe body behind a small Chrysler Hemi engine.

There has been a succession of hot rod and custom projects emerge from the Hadfield workshop since then. Meanwhile the T coupe project was progressing behind the scenes as the dream was still materialising in Rod's mind.

During that period Rod had the opportunity to purchase an all original 1919 T coupe body. The original '26 body was sent on its way and the pieces of the 1919 body were unloaded from the wooden box they came in and sent to Mark Rye for repair, replacement and renewal.

After the body was built a seamless tube chassis was started. The body was mounted on a large chassis table and with the engine (now updated to a Boss 429 Ford) jigged into position, work began on making the parts into a car.

The chassis is reminiscent of an early drag racing altered but superbly designed and welded to suit this application. A roll cage has been incorporated to maintain strength and help cope with the huge torque generated by the engine. The front end uses a stainless steel dropped axle with Holden stubs and a transverse spring. A Suzuki steering box operates through a hand built reversing mechanism. The front end also features a stainless steel stabiliser bar and Kawasaki brakes.

The rear end is a Halibrand quickchange with full floating axles to cope with the large offset wheels. Bilstein coil-over shockers provide the suspension and a hand made triangulated panhard bar is used to maintain lateral location with the four link system. Rear brakes are V8 Commodore while the emergency brake is a pinion mounted type. Wiring, brake and fuel lines are hidden in the chassis.

Hand built 16-inch wire spoke wheels at the front use Harley Davidson safety rims combined with custom made hubs and disc brake mounts. Tires are Avon 16x4 inch motorcycle type while the rear wheels are huge 16x15 inch US Indys with Mickey Thompson tires.

The engine is a 1968 Boss 429 Ford Hemi. The entire block was smoothed before George Haddad worked it over. The internals have been balanced and blueprinted and fitted with 7.5:1 pistons. A hand built oil pan covers the bottom end while a Crane camshaft operates Ford competition lifters and Boss pushrods. Cylinder heads remain stock and are topped with a hand built intake manifold that mounts two fully polished GM 6.71 blowers. More hand built artistry is revealed in the blower drive and the electronic injection system was also hidden inside the manifold.

Wellbaum built the brass radiator that incorporates a shroud for the electric fan. The exhaust system is stainless steel with mufflers hidden in the side pipes. Transmission is a Doug Nash 4+1 with a Hurst shifter.

House of Kolor Black was applied by Anton Degan and the interior is trimmed in red leather by Gavin Hill. Window frames, dash and steering wheel have been whittled from mahogany, the gauges are Classics and the column controls now operate the dip switch and turn signals.

Every nut, bolt and washer plus the majority of the fittings such as rod ends are stainless steel and most were custom made. Headlights and cowl lights are Model T items, brass or gold plated and converted to 12-volt. Power comes from two 12-volt batteries under the seat.

Rod credits the staff of the Castlemaine Rod Shop, those already mentioned in this article and the following: Complete Metal Finishers, Castle Hydraulics, Castle Auto Electrics, Ray Charlton, Pro-One Race Cars plus Bill Mussett and Trevor Shill for their individual efforts in designing and building many of the intricate parts of the car.

You could be excused for thinking this is only a show car that probably won't ever run. Take another look at the photos, see that discolouration of the exhaust, this is one radical show car that is fully functional. For Rod Hadfield, it's a dream come true.

Gordon Veal
1936 Chrysler Coupe
Annarbor, MI USA

Only a blown Hemi would be right for a radical '36 Chrysler coupe and that's what Gordon Veal fitted in the engine bay of his blue example. A tubbed rear end makes room for giant Mickey Thompson Sportsman tires on Weld wheels and there's a custom made alloy fuel tank nestled between the tubs in the trunk.

Inside the coupe, Gordon travels in comfort on two tone grey tweed upholstery and a set of RJ's competition belts keep him in place in the seat. Vehicle control comes in the form of a polished tilt column with Le Carra steering wheel, the vital functions are monitored by Stewart Warner gauges in an engine turned dash panel and the transmission is engaged with a Lokar shifter.

Jill & Roger Attwood
1939 Ford Convertible
Omaha, NE USA

What started out as a '39 Ford convertible Coast to Coast fiberglass body has been modified as much as possible to make it look not like a Coast to Coast body, but more like a one-off body style. Helping achieve that result are such custom fittings as Prowler headlights, a one-off grille, reshaped hood, reshaped and moulded front and rear fenders, a relocated rear license plate and rounded corners all over the body.

The frame is a modified Coast to Coast item with a new crossmember and different size coil-overs in the rear to get it lower. Aldan coil-overs are used for all suspension with a four link on the rear for location. The convertible has an LT1 engine with a fairly extensive custom made engine cover. It's backed by a 4L60E transmission and an eight inch Ford rear end that retains drum brakes.

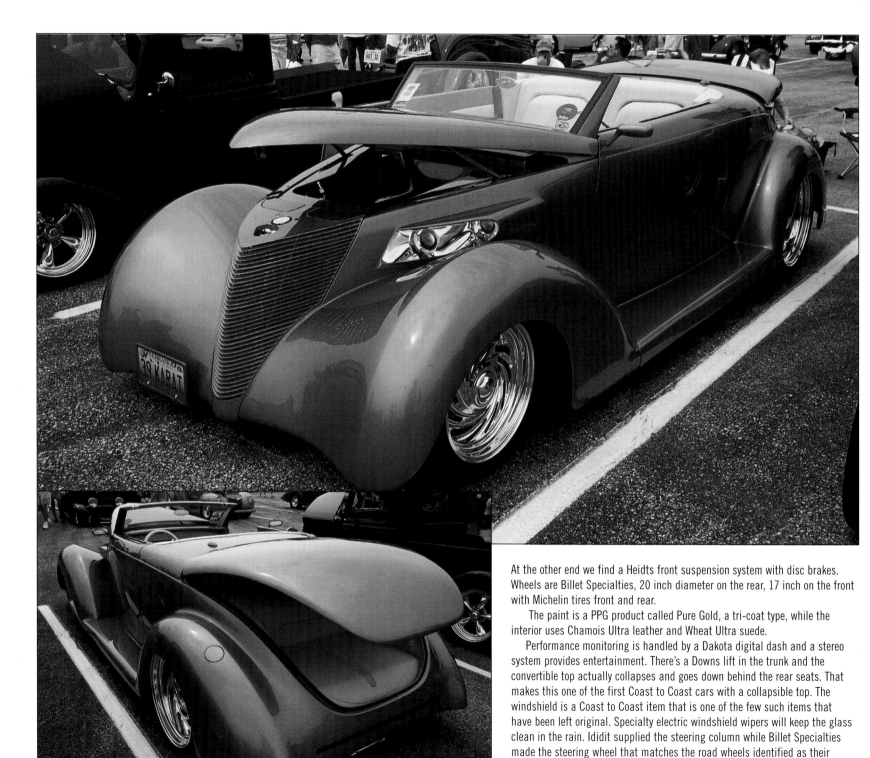

At the other end we find a Heidts front suspension system with disc brakes. Wheels are Billet Specialties, 20 inch diameter on the rear, 17 inch on the front with Michelin tires front and rear.

The paint is a PPG product called Pure Gold, a tri-coat type, while the interior uses Chamois Ultra leather and Wheat Ultra suede.

Performance monitoring is handled by a Dakota digital dash and a stereo system provides entertainment. There's a Downs lift in the trunk and the convertible top actually collapses and goes down behind the rear seats. That makes this one of the first Coast to Coast cars with a collapsible top. The windshield is a Coast to Coast item that is one of the few such items that have been left original. Specialty electric windshield wipers will keep the glass clean in the rain. Ididit supplied the steering column while Billet Specialties made the steering wheel that matches the road wheels identified as their Twister model.

Lifting the hood reveals a blown big block Chevy fed by twin four barrel carbs that dominates the engine bay of Hal Rasberry's awesome Willys. The rear view is equally dominant with huge tubs housing Mickey Thompson Sportsman tires wrapped around Budnik wheels. BF Goodrich Comp TAs are used on the front.

Interior trim features fawn leather with wool inserts, there's a set of Stewart Warner gauges in the dash and the driver controls the directions via a polished tilt column with Le Carra steering wheel. Passenger comfort is taken care of by air conditioning.

There's a Heidts Superide front suspension unit under the front of Greg Downhour's '34 Chevy cabriolet and a nine inch Ford rear end with four bar location and coil-over pro-street suspension at the rear. Nothing less than a 392 Hemi with 727 Torqueflite transmission provides the motive power for this cabriolet. A 3000 rpm stall speed converter is used in the transmission and a short tunnel ram with a pair of Edelbrock 650 carbs provides the induction for the Hemi. Moon valve covers dress up the engine exterior while inside there's been a .040" overbore. The reground hydraulic cam features .460" lift and a set of Sanderson headers have been Jet Hot coated for durability and appearance. Griffin supplied the radiator to cool the Hemi. A stainless steel exhaust system empties into a set of dump pipes at the rear.

Chassis for the Chevy came from Outlaw while Old Chicago made the body and grille. Headlights are unusual '27 Jordan items. The cabriolet retains its original style folding top while inside are burgundy leather Fiero seats, a tilt Billet Specialties alloy steering column and wheel, along with VDO gauges in the dash. Vintage Air air-conditioning keeps the passengers cool in Summer and a Kenwood radio and six disc changer provides the entertainment. The trunk is trimmed in leather in the same style as the rest of the interior.

Wheels are Billet Specialties Eagles, 15x10 and 15x6 fitted with Michelin tires. LED lights are featured all round for turn, brake and taillights.

Chris Soldatos is quite well known in the hot rod/drag racing scene, having built and raced a "wild, wheel standing" big block powered Model A coupe several years ago. A panel beater by trade, Chris is far too busy earning a living to spend precious time fiddling with project cars, so he enlisted the help of Leigh Charter to help him build his dream roadster. Body modifications include a revolutionary curved windshield – created by cutting the desired shape from a late model van windshield. This is framed by a set of Hi-Tech windscreen posts and billet mirrors. Seven inch wheel tubs out back are well filled by a set of 15x14 inch Center Line Convo-Pro rims running Mickey Thompson 15x29.5x18.5 fat rubber.

With the body modifications completed, Chris enlisted the staff at his own shop to prepare the body for that deep, glorious Timber Green paint – applied to perfection by Ernie. Inside, the roadster was trimmed in beige leather over an imported seat frame by Gavin Hill of Bendigo Trim. A filled dash features Auto Meter gauges and an IDIDIT column with a Budnik billet wheel. Ford commercial headlights retain the traditional hot rod flavor, as do teardrop taillights at the rear. A Hi-Tech grille insert completes the smooth exterior look of the roadster. All electrical wiring was sorted and installed by Jamie.

Underneath the shining exterior sits an aftermarket chassis with a stainless steel A-arm independent front end and Commodore steering. A Ford nine inch diff with Mark Williams LSD aluminum centre and 3.21:1 gears is supported by chrome-moly four bar suspension that uses Aldan Eagle shocks and springs. DBA disc brakes ensure adequate stopping power and are operated by a Hi-Tech pedal assembly.

Rudy Racing Engines built the supercharged 454 Chevy four bolt mains engine, that has been bored to 461 cubic inches and features a steel crankshaft, Engle con rods, TRW 8:1 blower pistons and moly rings. A high volume oil pump draws from a Hi-Energy pan, while a Crane roller cam and lifters are kept working by a Milodon gear drive. Aluminum 360 DART cylinder heads are kept flowing with $7/16$ inch Crower pushrods, while a 6/71 supercharger sucks fuel from a pair of 600 Holley double-pumpers. Spark is supplied by a Mallory 6-AL ignition system, while gases exit through a 'Mrs Hosmer' custom exhaust. An Aussie Desert Cooler radiator aided by twin thermatic fans keep engine heat to a minimum, while a T400 automatic transmission and Dominator torque converter wage a constant war with the horsepower flowing through the drive train. Gears are selected with a B&M Hammer style shifter.

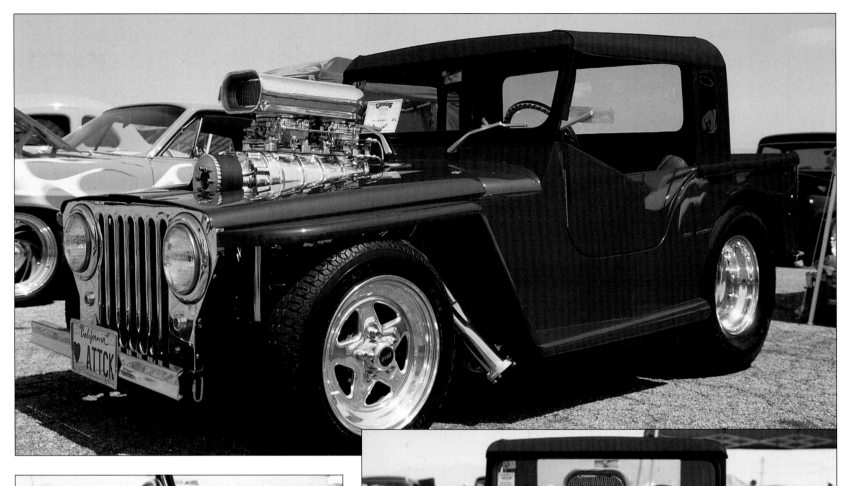

Paul Packham
1947 Willys CJ2a World War II Jeep.
California USA

Who would have thought a Jeep could fit into the world of Radical Hot Rods? Paul Packham, that's who. He took an original Jeep tub, lengthened the front fenders and engine compartment by 2½ inches and built up the cowl to give the vehicle a more aggressive stance and provide more space for the V8 running gear. The windshield was also chopped 2½ inches giving the Jeep an overall appearance like no other, yet it is still readily identifiable. The hood was custom made to suit the longer engine bay and the body remains all steel. A custom made top consists of Mercedes cloth over a custom made frame and the rear bumper was made from 12 pieces of metal with the LED lights included in the bar. A slot in the rear of the body houses a third brake light.

The engine is a destroked 400 cubic inch small block Chevy that now displaces 377 cubic inches and is topped with a 6.71 blower that is 12% underdriven. Keeping the internal temperature under control is an aluminum Trick-Flow radiator while an MSD ignition fires it into life. Transmission is Turbo 700R4 with 2800-rpm stall speed torque converter. Mustang II independent front suspension features stainless steel arms while the nine-inch rear end is narrowed and located by a four-link system with coil-over shock absorbers providing the suspension. Center gears are 3.89:1 with Posi-traction. Fuel is stored in a 27 gallon custom made tank.

The fireproof, anti-fade leather interior trim is the same as used on 747 planes and came from England. Dakota Digital gauges fill the dash, while Paul grips a Budnik steering wheel. Weld wheels carry 31x16.5 M&H rear tires that break loose at 60 mph when the right foot is planted. That's not surprising when you consider the Jeep only weighs 2300 pounds.

Garret and Vikki Kitchen
1948 Anglia
Groveport, OH USA

Garret Kitchen has been into hot rods since around the age of 13. While riding in a poker run with his pal Frank they saw an old beat up Anglia for sale. It had been a drag car and was a mess. The body had to be re-structured in order to mount it correctly on the chassis Garret built. Originally the engine had a regular carburetor set up on the motor but no real pro-street car comes without a blower so a BDS blower went on together with digital fuel injection.

Garret had problems finding someone to take on the difficult task of doing the sheet metal and body work so he ended up doing it himself, just from watching others and learning by trial and error.

Some of the body modifications that were done to the car include reversed opening power deck lid, power gas door, shaved door handles, hidden hinges, and power windows. These items also open by remote control. Garret molded a bead around the entire lower edge of the car, the rear wheel openings have

been raised and the fender openings have been changed, but still remain stock in width. This was done to show that an Anglia can be slammed in the rear and run 31 x 18.5 tires without running wider fenders. The taillight is a single lens with running, turn and brake light all in one. The turn signals are out of an early Cougar with the intermittent lighting pattern. The floors are all 304 stainless steel, all done in-house. This car will never rust.

The headliner was made of fiberglass using another Anglia, (real piece of junk) turned upside down. A mold was made first, then the final part. The speakers are in the headliner, two six inch and one ten inch in the rear and two tweeters up front. The stereo is a Clarion CD unit that is specially wired so that the face controller is separate from the main body and you insert the CD under the seat. The speaker grilles are machined billet aluminum in a slotted pattern that carries throughout most of the car.

Gerald and Geneva Lindsey
1937 Studebaker
Smithville, MO USA

You would never know it now but Gerald and Geneva Lindsey's '37 Studebaker was once a hump back four door sedan. The hump was removed and the rear doors welded shut to completely change the appearance of the sedan. Fenders were welded to the body, suicide doors were built, running boards custom made and the rear fenders extended down four inches. While the body was being worked over, the top was chopped three inches and the rear glass and surrounding panel laid forward three inches. The windshield was also slanted back to keep the top in proportion. Apart from the new slanted back, the body was treated to a custom made rear dovetail with exhaust cutouts incorporated. Prowler headlights give the frontal appearance an updated look while the original headlights were used to make the unusual engine cover. The stock grille was shortened and leaned back, vents were scalloped into the hood sides and all the corners rounded for a truly integrated appearance. The body has been channeled three inches over the frame. Windsor Fabrications supplied the custom built fuel access door. Finally the body was bathed in Cobalt Blue from House of Kolor.

Buried in the engine bay is a 454 Chevy that has been treated to a mild cam and rebuild and it is backed up by a Turbo 700R transmission with cable operated remote shifter. A Walker radiator keeps things cool in the engine bay while Vintage Air air conditioning does the same for the passengers. The rear end is a popular nine inch Ford item. Disc brakes are used front and rear and the suspension is a combination of Air Ride and Mustang II front end.

Inside there's a home built dash, filled with Dakota Digital instruments while the seats came from a '98 Intrepid. Entertainment is provided by a DVD player and TV. Bone leather and mauve tweed covers the seats. Custom door trims and the package tray at the back were custom built from wood and painted. The tilt-tele steering column is from a '76 Impala with Colorado Custom steering wheel attached. Tinted glass protects the interior and its occupants from the extremes of the climate and Dodge Neon third brake lights used as taillights alert other drivers when the eye-catching Studebaker is stopping. Colorado Custom 20x8 and 17x8 wheels carry Bridgestone 255/35/20 and 225/35/17 tires.

When was the last time you saw a Model T four door sedan that would qualify as a radical hot rod? Normally destined to the mundane restored car fraternity, Bill and Linda Miller have broken the mold with their Peptobismo Pink with Violet Pearl overlay version. What immediately draws your attention to this sedan is the huge 392 Chrysler Hemi stuffed into the engine bay with a Turbo 400 screwed to the back of the block. Even though the Hemi is stock, but for a pair of Edelbrock 600 carbies, the hood needed to be lengthened 15 inches to accommodate its physical size. Helping out in that regard underneath the T is a hand-made 2x4 box steel frame fitted out with a Dutchman rear end and a TCI independent front end. Dayton chrome wire wheels are 17x7 and 20x8 with Dunlop tires. The body and fenders are all original steel with the addition of a fuel filler door from a '75 American Motors vehicle and a third brake light from a Dodge Neon. A radiator was custom made to fit the confines of the T grille shell, that has a billet grille insert, and be efficient enough to cool the Hemi.

Power operated windows open to reveal an interior that features Intrepid front power seats and a Plymouth Horizon rear seat back rest with narrowed Pontiac Le Mans base, all covered in burgundy leather. Ididit supplied the steering column that wears a Le Carra wheel while Dakota Digital made the instruments that live in a hand carved wooden dash. A mini overhead console houses the Panasonic stereo CD while a small console on the floor provides a home for the ignition switch, headlight switch and power window switches. A Lincoln Continental provided the dome lights.

The Ida family have long been Willys enthusiasts and have built themselves quite a business specialising in building them for customers. Little wonder then that son Rob's own version of the popular '41 coupe would be a radical high end example of the breed that stops people in their tracks. This Willys coupe literally demands that you stop and pay attention.

First there is the radically low stance, then your eye drifts to the huge diameter custom made Bob Ida wheels with hidden mounting system and super low-profile tires. Once you get above them you will be dazzled by the House of Kolor Tangelo Pearl paint bathing the entire body that has many custom alterations including a lift out center section in the roof and curved windshield. Now if you take a glance under the custom tapered hood, there is more exotic engineering to take your breath away. Here we find a rare LT-5 Corvette engine that has been polished and detailed to perfection. The transmission is a ZF six speed from the same model Corvette that provided the engine.

Once your eyes refocus take a look inside and you will see pure white leather over Tea's Design seats. It all looks too clean to be used and it is teamed with a polished Billet Specialties tilt column topped with a one-off Bob Ida billet wheel. There's a DVD screen in the console and Auto Meter Ultra Light gauges centrally mounted in the dash for monitoring the vital functions of the coupe.

The coupe is mounted on a custom version of an Ida Automotive chassis with nine inch Ford based rear end that uses a billet center housing for the 4.11:1 gears and four link locating system. Front suspension is also Ida built, fully independent with billet A arms and four piston equipped calipers on the disc brakes.

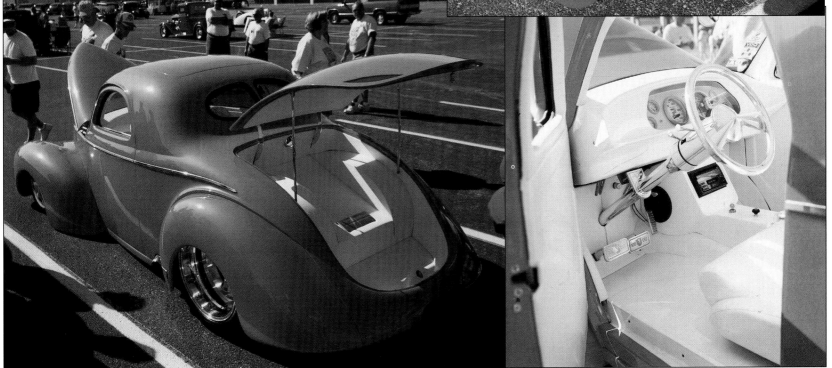

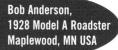

When you look at Bob Anderson's Model A roadster it is more what you don't see than what you do that makes it a radical hot rod. Hidden inside that Brookville body is a chrome moly $1\frac{5}{8}$ inch diameter tubing frame bent to follow the bottom of body. The front rails are '32 Chevy welded over the tube only where it extends forward from the firewall. A Super Bell axle with '42-48 Ford brakes and Buick drums lead at the front while Vega cross steer and Pete and Jake's shockers keep it under control. The rear end is a narrowed nine inch with Viper coil-overs. The project was somebody's cast off – so Bob doesn't have a lot of money in the car. Chassis tubing is built in backbone style that forms the tunnel within the car and gives it strength and rigidity.

The 392 Hemi engine has been rebuilt and balanced and is topped with six Rochester two barrels on an Edelbrock intake. The distributor is stock with electronic conversion. Home made

headers were chromed and fitted with motorcycle baffles. A Griffin radiator was made to a template and is assisted by electric and mechanical fans. Transmission is a rebuilt but standard 727 Torqueflite.

The Brookville steel body was cut through the door area and lengthened slightly to allow flush mount doors. Rear wheel well radius has been filled to follow the tire diameter and the lower edge of the body extended two inches and molded to the chassis tube. A lower floor pan underneath hides the round tube frame from view and the body has full floor depth despite the channeled appearance. Tilting the seat forward reveals the custom made gas tank. Inside there's a false floor welded in as well, but wiring and plumbing is hidden in between. The hollow toe board is used to route wiring etc. to the engine. A back seat from a Pinto wagon has been modified and retrimmed in white vinyl with black cut-pile carpet on the floor. Shifter is a cable drive item from a Corvette. Stewart Warner gauges under the dash are the only ones that work. The dash is from a '50 Olds, shortened to suit and enhanced with a '61 Buick steering wheel. Two inches were chopped from the windshield and the top of the posts rounded and welded on. No top is used, the only protection being the chromed roll bar. At the rear the body reveal was welded to an extended body with brake tube

used to form its shape that incorporates '58 Belair taillights, the first items bought for the car.

Wheels are Chevy steels, the axle bolt patterns have been changed to the caps are '50s style sunburst. Tires are Firestone 5.90x15 conventionals on the front and 7.60x15 on the rear. House of Kolor Candy Organic Green paint was applied over a green base. The trunk has been trimmed to match the interior.

That headlight and grille pod has '62 Thunderbird lights and a stainless steel insert made from sewer filter grille. It's a repro fiberglass surround by Jezak Promotions as used in the sixties, but modified at the rear edges with fiberglass to suit this installation.

Van Tyler had Alloway Hot Rod Shop of Knoxville TN put together this radical '33 Ford roadster that is powered by an Alloy head equipped 454 big block Chevrolet with Turbo 700R transmission. A chromed Super Bell dropped axle front end is held in place by a four bar and features Posie's spring along with Wilwood disc brakes. At the other end is a Winters quick-change rear end fitted with 4.17:1 and 3.88:1 gears. It is also held in place by a four bar with coil-over shock absorbers for suspension.

The body came from Rat's Glass and has been superbly drenched in '96-'97 Corvette Grand Am Blue with flames by Roehl and Hughes. Running boards have been painted to match the body and the taillight staunchions have been shortened. Frontal appearance has been enhanced by the use of '34 Ford commercial headlights and a chromed grille insert. The paint scheme is brilliantly set off by polished 15x4½ and 16x9½ American Racing five spoke wheels fitted with Michelin 135/15 and 265/75/16 tires.

Separating the passengers from the elements is a Duval style windshield while inside they sit on red leather trim by Paul Atkins that carries through to the trunk. A flat spoke wheel tops an Ididit tilt steering column while the driver monitors vital functions via Auto Meter gauges. Lokar made the shifter and pedals.

Steve Grimes has a penchant for the unusual when it comes to hot rods so it's no surprise to find he built most of the parts for his T Trackster. You can't buy these things in kit form so Steve built the frame himself and used a V8-60 Flathead Ford motor. He wanted to make it look like one of these old hot rods that used to take the radiator off and run the water through the block. Steve went to the trouble of running the water down through the frame to a radiator at the rear and then back into the frame. The car uses a little roadster body that Steve cut down and he made a top for it using an aluminum frame with aluminum sheet over that, pop riveted on and then just covered with top material. He wanted something very rigid and it hinges on the front so he can get in and out easily.

Suspension on the front uses a Moredrop Model A axle with quarter elliptic springs, friction shocks and hairpin radius rods, all made by

Steve. Steering box is from an early '70s Dodge with a modified pitman arm. The '35 Ford wire wheels were widened for the back and bolted to a stock '36 Ford rear end. In fact the entire drive train is pretty much stock featuring a torque-tube drive that has been shortened and a three-speed manual transmission that, being from a V8-60, is different from the normal 85hp full-size Ford version. Tires are 235/85/R16.

The engine features radical looking straight header pipes into which Steve fitted Harley Davidson motorcycle baffles and he put little VW tips on the ends just to hold them in place. It runs surprisingly quiet. Stromberg 81 carburetors feed the V8-60, that has Edelbrock heads and stock ignition that is converted to 12 volt. Model A taillights are used along with a taillight over the license plate that has a red dot over a blue light, a flea market thing that Steve thinks might be from a motorcycle.

With tongue firmly pressed into his cheek Steve proclaims that the T is sponsored by the Blue Moon Burlesque House that currently stars Bubbles Laroo and the Boom Boom Girls at 2637 Wilshire Boulevard, Palm Grove, California. Why not drive down there and see the T parked out front?

**Dave and Lori Jordan
1932 Zipper Roadster
Lake Ozark, MO USA**

The swoopy reproduction fiberglass body used on Dave Jordan's flamed roadster is a '32 Ford Zipper. It has a removable hard top, custom dash, a lot of one-off features including a steering wheel and rear view mirror. Dave and his wife operate Dave's Rod Shop where all of the work was completed. Custom taillights were made up as was a custom exhaust system that has two exhausts running into one outlet at the back. A front "cowl catcher" features built-in custom turn signals. Dupont base coat/clear coat flames go down the '33 style fenders. Apparently Zipper had 35 roadsters like this and they sold a fender package, but Dan has never seen another one with fenders on it. Most of them came out as a regular hiboy. The fenders have been widened a further two inches giving the roadster a truly unique appearance.

The roadster is powered by a 383 Chevy stroker, that produces 450 horsepower and 495 foot pounds of torque. A Turbo 350 transmission drives to a Ford nine inch rear end sporting 3.50:1 gears and located by a four link. There's a Heidts Super-ride front end nestled under the front with stainless steel arms and the wheels are American Torq-Thrusts with Sun Specs custom one-off billet factory built center caps.

The interior is leather, gauges are Dolphins in a custom dash and there's leather on the floors. More leather graces the rest of the interior and trunk with rosewood trim used as highlights. The top is a lift-off hard top that's covered in canvas.

**Kevin and Karen Alstott
1932 Boydster
Ft Dodge, IA USA**

Thanks to the people at Boyd Coddington garage, radical hot rods are now more accessible to any hot rodder. Their new reproduction Boydster kit comes as a rolling project that you can modify and outfit to suit your own tastes, with much of the major work already done. This particular car was one of the first to be released and Kevin says it was relatively easy to put together. One of the things he did change was to put 20-inch diameter Boyd Coddington Fury wheels on the rear so the fenders were stepped and widened and the running board stepped out to meet the fenders. Those wheels are 10 inches wide on the back with 295/40 Goodyear tires and 18-inch diameter on the front with 215/40 tires.

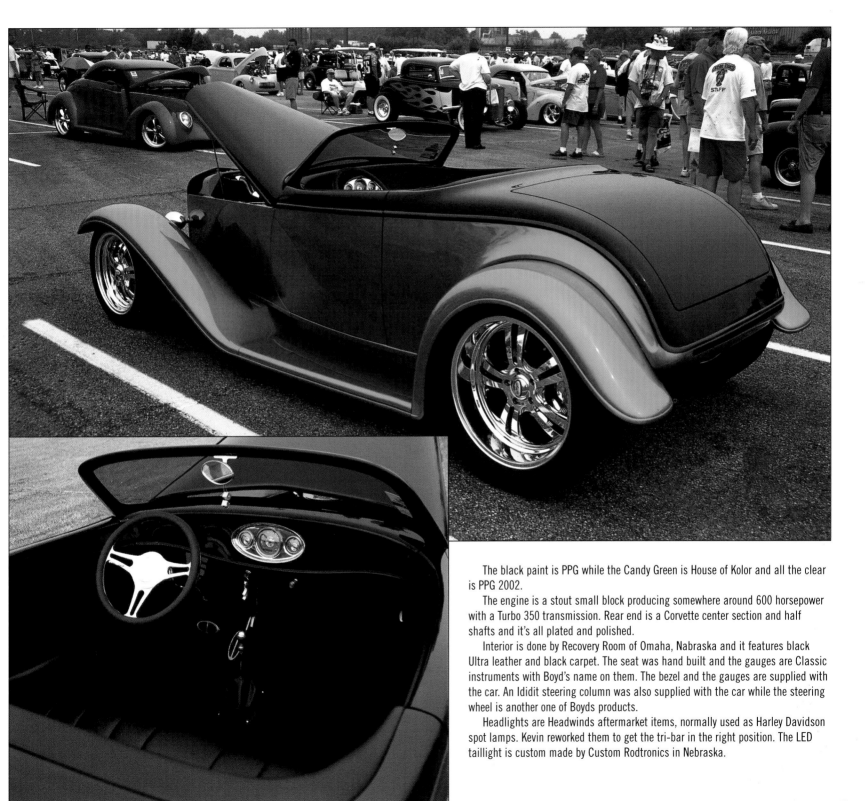

The black paint is PPG while the Candy Green is House of Kolor and all the clear is PPG 2002.

The engine is a stout small block producing somewhere around 600 horsepower with a Turbo 350 transmission. Rear end is a Corvette center section and half shafts and it's all plated and polished.

Interior is done by Recovery Room of Omaha, Nabraska and it features black Ultra leather and black carpet. The seat was hand built and the gauges are Classic instruments with Boyd's name on them. The bezel and the gauges are supplied with the car. An Ididit steering column was also supplied with the car while the steering wheel is another one of Boyds products.

Headlights are Headwinds aftermarket items, normally used as Harley Davidson spot lamps. Kevin reworked them to get the tri-bar in the right position. The LED taillight is custom made by Custom Rodtronics in Nebraska.

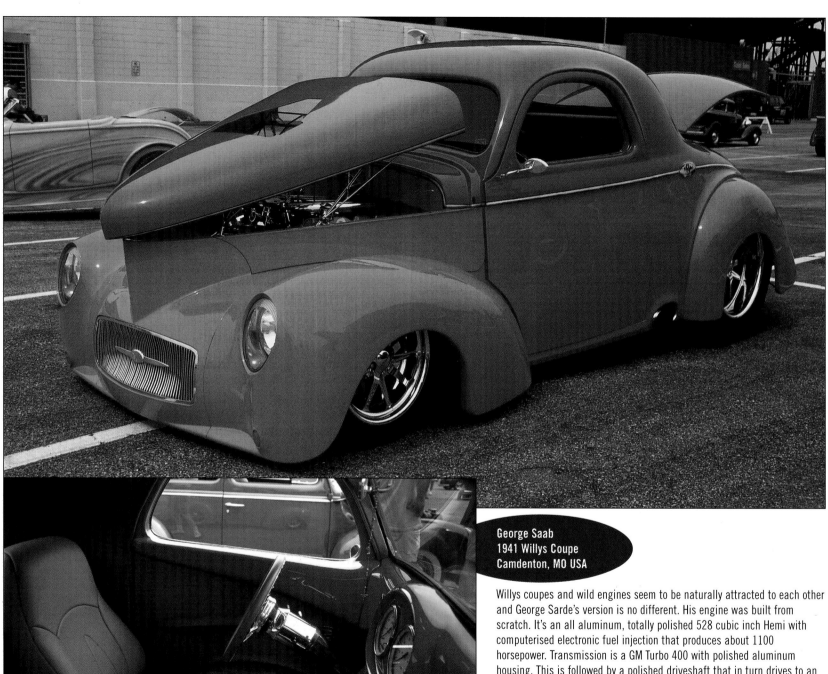

George Saab
1941 Willys Coupe
Camdenton, MO USA

Willys coupes and wild engines seem to be naturally attracted to each other and George Sarde's version is no different. His engine was built from scratch. It's an all aluminum, totally polished 528 cubic inch Hemi with computerised electronic fuel injection that produces about 1100 horsepower. Transmission is a GM Turbo 400 with polished aluminum housing. This is followed by a polished driveshaft that in turn drives to an all chrome Kugel third member located by a stainless steel four-link. The housing is a one-only built from scratch. Front and rear suspension make use of Air-Ride Technologies components and the Budnik wheels are 17 inch on the front and 20 inch on the rear fitted with Toyo tires. Front end is a Mustang II.

Body is from Dennis Taylor and George is very pleased with this high quality body. Headlights are custom made by Dave Jordan using Juliano '39

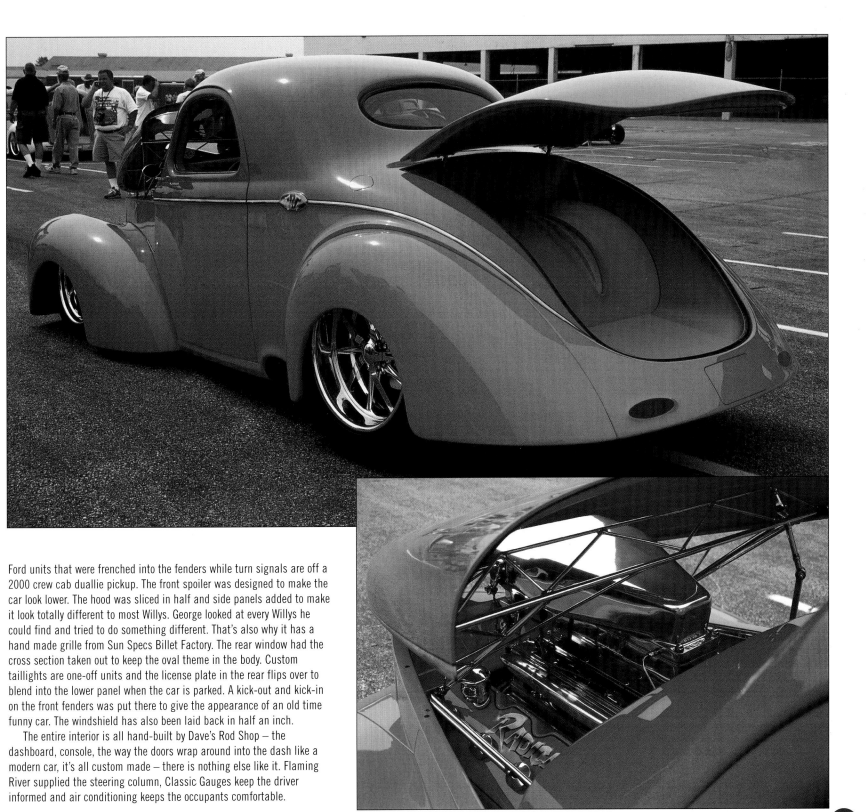

Ford units that were frenched into the fenders while turn signals are off a 2000 crew cab duallie pickup. The front spoiler was designed to make the car look lower. The hood was sliced in half and side panels added to make it look totally different to most Willys. George looked at every Willys he could find and tried to do something different. That's also why it has a hand made grille from Sun Specs Billet Factory. The rear window had the cross section taken out to keep the oval theme in the body. Custom taillights are one-off units and the license plate in the rear flips over to blend into the lower panel when the car is parked. A kick-out and kick-in on the front fenders was put there to give the appearance of an old time funny car. The windshield has also been laid back in half an inch.

The entire interior is all hand-built by Dave's Rod Shop – the dashboard, console, the way the doors wrap around into the dash like a modern car, it's all custom made – there is nothing else like it. Flaming River supplied the steering column, Classic Gauges keep the driver informed and air conditioning keeps the occupants comfortable.

Boyd Coddington says he always wanted to build an all aluminum car. On this project he started out building a '29 Model A pickup, but as the project progressed it got to change to a style somewhere between a '29 and a '30. Boyd's crew worked together with Marcel and his sons on the body with all the sheet metal fabrication, aluminum machine work and fabrication done in Boyd's shop.

Even the frame is made from aluminum as is the front axle, which is whittled from 60-61 aluminum and the spindles are 20-24. The brakes are all aluminum too and the rear end is an aluminum Winters quick change.

An aluminum GM block formed the basis of the Chevy engine that is topped with a pair of factory aluminum heads and capped below with a machined aluminum oil pan. A Fel-Pro computer runs the whole Enderle injection system. The stacks for the fuel injection were all custom made and all the bell cranks were remachined. A Meziere remote water pump was used as Boyd tried to keep a race car theme throughout, walking the fine line between nostalgia and high tech. Boyd says he wanted to do something that people would really appreciate; looking at it as a Model A pickup truck, all filled out in aluminum with the application of modern technology.

The interior is in silver naugahyde to match the aluminum color. When first started the truck was intended to end up painted in either orange or black but everyone likes it too much as is, so it probably won't be painted now – the natural aluminum color is going to be retained. Gabe Lopez did the interior trim and made the aluminum steering column, all aluminum pedals and aluminum insert.

Wheels are special one-off Boyd Coddington, 15s on the front and 17s on the rear with 255/55/17s Goodyear tires on the back, 155/55/15 Goodyears on the front.

Shane Weckerly
1940 Willys Two Door Sedan
Chino Hills, CA USA

A lot of Willys coupes are featured in this book. Let's face it, they have a way of attracting the high performance hot rodder. But there's only one '40 Willys two door sedan and it didn't even start out that way. Shane engaged John Cambria to help him convert the body from four door to two door configuration and they also modified it to accept a '37 deck lid. A new floor was fabricated to fit around the tubbed chassis.

The chassis was fabricated from 2x4 inch rectangular tubing and equipped with a 10-point roll cage. Under the front is a Mustang II front end with dropped spindles. A narrowed nine inch on Aldan coil-overs is held in place by a four link at the rear and it is equipped with a Moser spool and 35 spline axles. They're needed to absorb the torque from a blown 392 Chrysler Hemi engine bolted to a 727 Torqueflite trans with Cheetah manual valve body and 3500 rpm stall speed converter. Cooling is provided by an aluminum radiator. Grey nylon interior trim covers Procar racing bucket seats and German wool carpets are used on the floor. The stock dash holds Auto Meter gauges and the steering column is topped witha Superior Industries wheel.

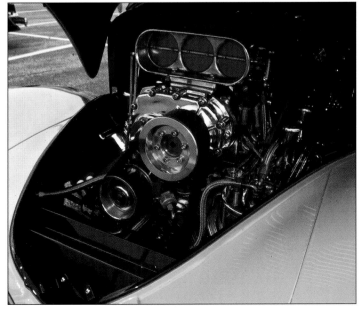

No, Ron Hassell hasn't found a unique American made '37 Ford roadster, and it isn't one of the roadsters made in Australia during that period. Ron's roadster was made from a Minotti fiberglass coupe body with the top removed.

While the body was being rearranged the doors were made to open in suicide fashion and a billet horizontal bar grille by Don's Hot Rods was incorporated. Custom bumperettes add fine detail and they have been pulled close in to the body. The windshield was specially designed off a mold and it's made from poly-carbonate as they use in Nascar racing now. This is brand new material and they hadn't even started using it at the time Ron's roadster was built. More one-off parts used on the car are the Boyd Coddington wheels that are 20 inch diameter on the back and 17 inch on the front.

Underneath the roadster is all '99 Corvette running gear that had to be lengthened seven-inches and narrowed four-inches. The 2001 LS6 fuel injected Corvette engine was also used and it puts out 450 hp, gets over 27 mile per gallon as is, and uses a carbon fiber drive shaft. Three inch stainless exhausts are coated inside and out. The running gear is all mounted in a 3/16 inch chrome moly frame with Air Ride Technology suspension all the way around. It only takes about three seconds to set it to ride height ready to go. Ron claims he has over 6,000 hours invested in the car.

Interior trim was done by Paul Atkins in caramel leather over Lexus seats that were pirated from a new Lexus coupe that had been rolled. The dash is from a Prowler.

Bob Lowe
1932 Ford Hiboy Roadster
Springfield, MO USA

Bob Lowe's hiboy roadster started out as a Harwood body on which the rear wheel wells were raised two-inches and the rear pans sectioned $1\frac{3}{4}$ inches to keep it all proportional. The frame is a one-off that was 14 months in construction. Figuring out all the geometry involved in the suspension was time consuming but well worth the effort. All the fuel-lines, air-lines and brake-lines are hidden inside the frame rails. The frame rail lower reveal starts and actually narrows all the way to the front. Ladder bars for the rear end are enclosed inside the frame rail and the rear suspension uses Shockwaves, mounted parallel to the frame in front of the rear end and then cantilevered for their actuation. Crossmembers are all pressure tested and they act as the air-tanks for the air controlled suspension. The front end uses Air-Ride Technologies air-bags with a solid axle. Only two lower control arms are visible in the front as the upper four bars are triangulated inside the engine compartment.

The headlight buckets are all hand made as Bob thinned the grille shell and then felt the '34 commercial headlights needed to be thinned to match. They're hand made with the mounting bezels actually made out of a solid chunk of billet. These are made so that they actually screw into the buckets leaving no visible attachments.

Engine for the project is an LS6 Chevy that Bob bought eight years ago as a crate motor. He was going to use it in a '33 Willys hiboy, but discarded the project in favor of the Deuce. It features 11.2:1 compression, flowed heads, big valves and a Comp hydraulic cam, done especially for this application. Injection is an Enderle eight-stack that was built on a NOS Enderle manifold that Bob found at the Pomona swap meet. Greg Railsback of PBS designed and made all the electronic controls for the injection and all the injector tubes are hand made. Transmission is a Richmond six speed that drives to a Richmond Champ quick change rear end.

Gauges are Avionics dual reading control, apart from the speedo and the tach which is mounted down below. They have all been refaced with the name of the car and the color of the car. The dash arch was all done by Kurt Cunningham of the Carriage Works, who also did the steering wheel. Mirrors are hand made, the windshield is one of Jerry Kugel's curved, Duval styled items, made to suit the cowl of this car. Paul Atkins did the leather interior trim and covered the top, which is actually a lift-off aluminum item, with Harts cloth. Paint color is Merlowe to coincide with the owner's last name, it's a dark, dark wine color that most people think is actually black. The paint is a combination of two different company's products, House of Kolor and Glasurit.

Wheels are 15x7 and 17x10 inch Colorado Customs with extra details ball-milled into them and fitted with Goodrich and Michelin tires. The hubs of the wheels were also cut down to match the mating hubs on the axles. Little custom details like that are evident over the whole roadster.

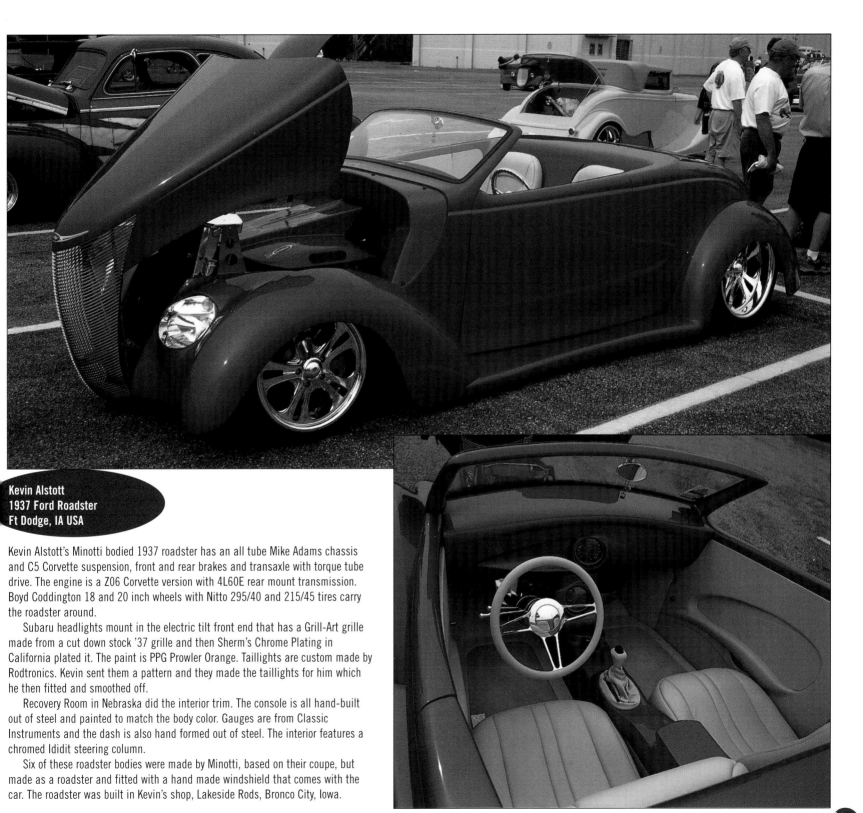

Kevin Alstott
1937 Ford Roadster
Ft Dodge, IA USA

Kevin Alstott's Minotti bodied 1937 roadster has an all tube Mike Adams chassis and C5 Corvette suspension, front and rear brakes and transaxle with torque tube drive. The engine is a Z06 Corvette version with 4L60E rear mount transmission. Boyd Coddington 18 and 20 inch wheels with Nitto 295/40 and 215/45 tires carry the roadster around.

Subaru headlights mount in the electric tilt front end that has a Grill-Art grille made from a cut down stock '37 grille and then Sherm's Chrome Plating in California plated it. The paint is PPG Prowler Orange. Taillights are custom made by Rodtronics. Kevin sent them a pattern and they made the taillights for him which he then fitted and smoothed off.

Recovery Room in Nebraska did the interior trim. The console is all hand-built out of steel and painted to match the body color. Gauges are from Classic Instruments and the dash is also hand formed out of steel. The interior features a chromed Ididit steering column.

Six of these roadster bodies were made by Minotti, based on their coupe, but made as a roadster and fitted with a hand made windshield that comes with the car. The roadster was built in Kevin's shop, Lakeside Rods, Bronco City, Iowa.

When he undertook this woody project Bob Johnson started out with a particular concept in mind. He wanted to reduce the excess wood bulk from body style and get more of the steel sedan look into it. To put that concept into play more curvature was designed into all the wood sections on the car and all the edges were radiused to visually soften up the hard maple wood used for the body.

The chassis under the car uses the original frame rails with '97 Lincoln Mark VIII independent rear end components. The center section, hub carriers and CV axles from the Lincoln were retained but tubular control arms, a billet cover and rear third member holder were custom made for this application. Air-Ride Shock Waves provide the suspension at the front and rear. Front suspension is based on a Mustang II and there are Nascar style sway bars front and rear. Baers four piston calipers grab 13½ and 14½ inch rotors at the

front and rear respectively. Hot Rodder custom wheels are 18x7 inch diameter on the front and 18x9½ inch on the rear with Michelin tires.

Powering the woody is a '98 Mustang Cobra engine, one of the modular 4.6 Ford motors with a Lincoln automatic transmission. Bob made a new upper intake for the car to relocate the throttle body to the front where it is part of a fresh air induction system. Almost everything else on the engine is for dress-up purposes only.

Paul Atkins from Colman, Alabama trimmed the interior using mid-eighties Mercedes roadster seats in the front, and a matching custom built rear. The dash was hand fabricated using original trim pieces modified and turned upside down. Classic Instruments gauges keep the driver informed, an Eclipse sound system provides entertainment and there's a DVD player and LCD screen in the dash, all mounted so they fold up into the dash where you don't see them if you don't want them on. Steering column is a Flaming River item and the steering wheel is from Colorado Custom. All the work was carried out at Bob's own business, Johnson's Hot Rod Shop, Gadstone, Alabama.

You won't find a more radical '37 Ford coupe than this one owned by Vern Rempfer. The steel body has been sectioned three inches and the top has been chopped three inches. That wasn't as straightforward as it sounds because in the process the top was moved forward to take out the side quarter windows. Sedan doors were shortened and made suicide opening style. The hood was extended, the grille sectioned and the custom made high density discharge headlights laid back. The trunk lid is one of the few parts of the body that was left factory standard when the rear bodyline was recontoured. It is now much different to a regular '37 Ford and has custom made taillights as well.

Underneath is a tubular chassis with suspension that features Air-Ride Shock Waves back and front. The rear end is the rodder's favorite, a standard nine-inch Ford with four link. Front suspension is based on a Mustang II unit and everything underneath is chromed. Wheels are Boyd Coddington 14x18s on the back and 17x7s on the front with Michelin tires.

That trick hood uses a power tilt up and forward mechanism to reveal a 502 Ramjet big block engine, the first one that was produced, and it has been all chromed and polished by the suppliers, Street & Performance.

Transmission is a robust Turbo 400, again all polished, as is the chrome third member. Exhaust features two-inch primary tubes coming out of the motor, going through the fender wells and then straight back into three-inch exhaust pipes with stainless steel mufflers.

All steel construction extends even to the interior to include the dash and all the interior sculpting. The driver gets to use a Lokar shifter, Ididit steering column with Budnik gasser wheel and Dakota digital gauges monitor performance functions. Seats are BMW, and the trim is finished in Ultra leather.

Chris Palazzo
1934 Ford Roadster
Bow Bowing, NSW Australia

Black paint with flames always has a way of grabbing your attention and there's no denying the competition feel afforded by the 12 spoke wheels at the front and those huge magnesium Halibrands at the rear of Chris Palazzo's roadster. But there's no radiator! That Chrysler Hemi uses methanol fuel which runs much cooler than gasoline, so it can be driven enough to wow the crowds at the shows and closed events where this roadster will spend most of its "road time".

The purchase of a Deuce Customs body and a Rod City chassis with independent front end started the project. Then a mate decided not to go ahead with a Wild Bunch drag racer and offered the engine to Chris. The chassis that forms the basis of the car has a four bar rear suspension system that utilises Aldan coil-overs to suspend a massive Winters/Richmond Champ diff with 4.11 gears and a locker spool and full floating hubs by Craft Diffs. A Commodore gave up its rack and pinion steering for the roadster and it is hooked to a Peter Laverty Engineering billet column. The 15 inch diameter spindle mount 12 spokers at the front have custom built knock off adaptors and are fitted with Michelin 135 tyres while the rear wheels are 16 inch with 345/55x16 BF Goodrich tyres.

John Kuiper Race Engines worked their magic on the 392 Hemi adding Mickey Thompson con rods and Venolia blower pistons, a Howard roller cam and an 8.71 blower

with Enderle injection. A manually shifted Turbo 400 auto trans has Hurst Quarterstick shifter and a Dominator 4,500 rpm stall speed converter. Steve Anderson and Liverpool Exhausts combined to produce the 2½ inch diameter zoomy headers.

The body has been channeled two inches over the frame with rake built in and the dash and upper doors have been remolded so that they flow into each other. At the rear a beaver panel has been added with sunken Caddy taillights while the windscreen frame is a custom made piece to suit the cut down Honda Civic windshield. Mike Gregorace of Bonnyrigg Smash Repairs was called on to lay on the deep Midnight Black paint before Chris turned his own graphic designer talents to applying the flames. Rod Lingard trimmed the interior in leather with Mercedes carpet on the floor. The dash might at first look plain but blended into it is a set of Dakota Digital gauges.

Those bug-eye headlights are Vintique reproductions and all the chrome was applied by Blu-Chrome. The fancy milled grille supports were machined by Frank at Express Tooling who was also responsible for the backing plates and knock-off adaptors. Chris wanted a car that had the killer stance and the power to back it up. He certainly got both and ended up with one of Australia's most incredible hot rods.

Mike Norton's '37 Cord looks radical because it started out as a '37 Westchester four-door sedan that has been shortened nine inches in the rear door area. The window area was blanked off to give a Le Baron style to the body and the front was lengthened the same amount as the rear was shortened. The top was chopped three inches and those smooth skirts started as '39 Ford items that have all been modified to look the same front and rear on their home made pods. Suspension covers are also home made items. They hide all Jaguar sedan suspension. Power comes from a TPI Camaro 350/350 combination with Walker radiator and polished stainless steel exhaust system. Inside are seats from a late model Jaguar Vanden Plas, with mahogany wood trim. Auto Meter Ultra Lite (Nascar) gauges fill the dash and storage area has been included under the rear floor and in the trunk. Detail paint on the interior window trims features two tone colours in orange and cream. This is a true home-built radical hot rod, painted under the carport in PPG orange mixing color base coat/clear coat. The Cord also features flush-fit windshield, electrically heated seats, keyless entry and ignition switching.

Niclas Adolfsson
1939 Ford Convertible
Nassjo, Sweden

Niclas Adolfsson's Swedish built '39 Ford Convertible was voted "Street Rod of the Year 2000". But it didn't start out as a convertible at all, he built it from a sedan!

In the spring of '87, after reading American rod and custom magazines since the early '80s, it struck Niclas that he should build his own rod. Niclas found a '39 Ford four sedan in a small village three hours south of his hometown. The car was complete but in a terrible condition, a true rust bucket, but it did fit Niclas' budget so he bought it.

After a closer inspection of the car Niclas discovered that the frame was broken in a few places by rust and that parts of the body were beyond repair. He soon realized that he would not be driving a low budget built street rod the following summer.

On giving it some serious thought he decided to turn the four-door sedan into a convertible. Almost the entire rear end of the body was in need of replacement with new steel anyway so why bother fixing it?

After Niclas had worked on the chassis for quite some time, adding a heavily modified Ford nine inch rear end and Mustang II front end with his own A-arms, his garage buddy Magnus Palm stopped him from improving the quality of his work any further – he was driving Magnus nuts!

Once Niclas started on the body it did not take long before he was driving Magnus nuts again. He changed the design of the windshield and frame three times before he was happy with it! An '87 Ford Escort convertible top was modified to fit the '39. It took weeks and there is almost nothing left of the Escort top. He also built three dashboards before he was pleased with the design that was inspired by early Corvettes.

Niclas wanted to achieve a smoother and somewhat "flattened" look with the body modifications. Rear fenders, trunk-lid and beaver panel were so rusty that they couldn't be fixed. Niclas got hold of parts in much better condition at Carlisle and the swap meet at Englishtown, NJ. A new floor was made from 1.25-mm sheet metal. The fenders are the least modified body pieces on the car, only the fender well 'lips' have been massaged and moved inwards. The lower part of the doors is extended to fill the stock gap between the door and running board. The doors are extended 35 mm in the front end.

Door handles were shaved, hood and firewall sectioned two inches, the hood was also 'pancaked', the upper peek of the hood is now 10 cm lower than stock and the owner made chrome strip in the middle of the grille continues onto the hood. Paint colour is Chrysler Wildberry Pearl by Bengt Alm at Alm's Body and Paint.

Niclas designed the interior himself and did all the work with the exception of the paint and upholstery. A custom instrument panel was used with Auto Meter Arctic White gauges and there's a leather covered Billet Specialties steering wheel on an Ididit Billet tilt steering column. A Lokar billet shifter resides in the custom floor console while the heater and power steering are hidden behind the instrument panel. Modified Honda Prelude '88 seats have had their head rests removed and the back of the seat is extended four centimetres.

Interior and trunk are covered with cream/yellow leather and fabric while leather covered aluminum sheet fills the area behind the seats. The inside of the doors have sculptured 10 cm polyester-plastic covered with fiberglass and leather, plus inserts of painted fiberglass, Volvo V70 '98 remote door locks, inside door handles made of 20x30 mm solid metal by the owner, chrome trim on the lower part of the door made by the owner and Juliano's seat belts hidden in the body next to the upper bar of the seats. An Optima battery is hidden behind the passenger seat. There's a Rock Valley 60-liter gas tank under the trunk floor. Entertainment is provided by a Sony Stereo with CD player in a hidden compartment under the left part of the instrument panel.

A chassis from Art Morrison, outfitted with Air-Ride suspension, forms the basis for Jim Stark's '37 Chevy delivery. The top was chopped three inches in the front and one inch at the back and the back door leaned in. Jim dropped the grille down an inch and a half and raked it back four inches. The front fenders were also cut down and rolled around about an extra four inches. To finish off the frontal appearance improvements Tony welded the one-piece hood together and cut louvers in the side grille panels to match the front grille. Adding to the refined styling is a one-piece late model Bronco windshield.

To complete the bodywork Tony rebuilt the firewall so it would clear the 502 Ramjet motor. Boyd Coddington 20 inch wheels are used on the back and 17 inch in front, with 295 and 235 tires at the rear and front respectively. A nine inch Ford rear end has 3.55 gears, while the

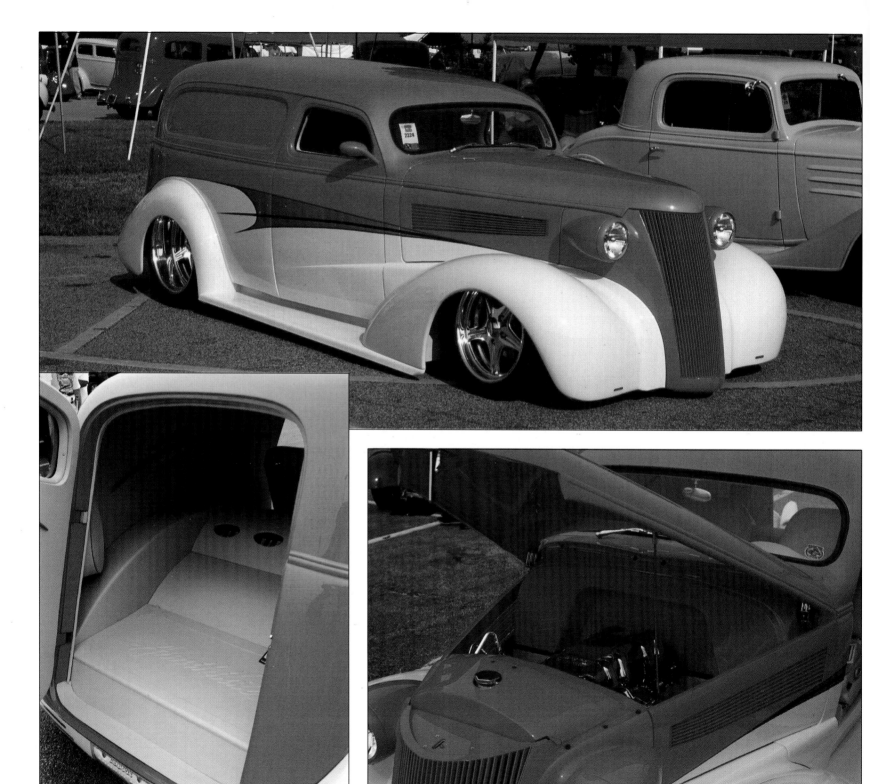

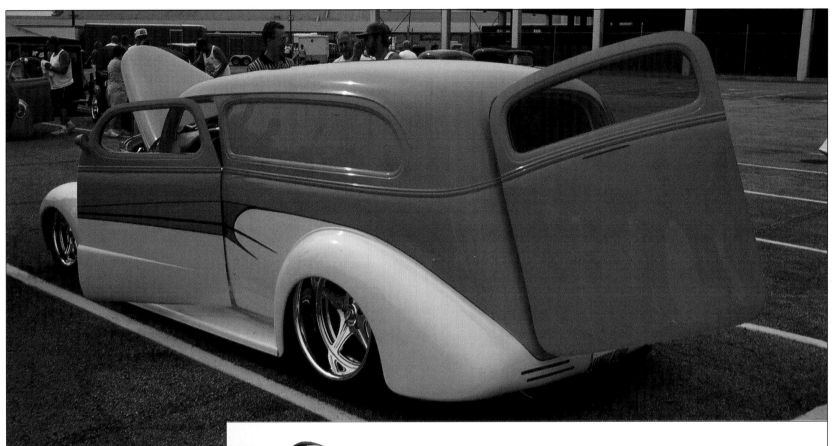

front end is based on a Mustang II unit. Brakes are Wilwood discs on all four corners.

The interior is finished in Ultra leather by Vintage Fabrication and it's got an Alpine stereo for entertainment. Steering wheel came from the Carriage Works out of Grandview. VDO gauges live in the dash and Vintage Air makes hot weather driving more comfortable. The two-tone paint is PPG Tangelo on the top half with Frost Beige on the bottom.

Doug Miller
1934 Chevy Coupe
Baton Rouge, LA USA

Stuffed in the engine bay of Doug Miller's '34 Chevy coupe is nothing less than a blown big block 427 Chevy equipped with twin four barrel carbs and a Turbo 350 transmission. Billet Specialties wheels carry the coupe to the rod runs on Mickey Thompson Sportsman tires at the rear and BF Goodrich Touring TAs at the front.

A Currie prepared nine inch rear end has coil-over suspension and four link locating system plus wheelie bars protruding from the rear. Heidts independent front suspension makes the driving easy and Wilwood four wheel disc brakes haul the coupe down from highway speeds.

Externally the top has been chopped and the headlights are now King Bees with H4 halogen inserts. Milled wipers keep the rain off the windshield. Inside there's grey leather trim with grey tweed inserts and magenta highlights. Milled dash inserts hold the gauges while passenger entertainment and comfort is taken care of by an Alpine sound system and air-conditioning.

JW & Ginger Williams
1939 Ford Two Door Sedan
Melbourne Beach, FL USA

Take a standard '39 Ford two door sedan, radically rework the body and it takes on a whole new appearance. The roof of the sedan has been chopped 2½ inches and made into a hard top with the center post removed. The body has also been sectioned 2½ inches, channeled 2½ inches and treated to reshaped fenders with Mercedes Benz headlights. Custom made belt moldings add a highlight to the Candy Red paintwork that was completed at Mike's Auto Body of Melbourne, Florida. The interior is full leather with mahogany accents.

Providing the motive power for the Tudor is an aluminum 4.6L Cobra engine that has been polished and dressed so you can barely recognise it. A polished five speed transmission transfers the power to the rear end and a polished stainless steel exhaust gets rid of waste gases. Four-wheel disc brakes improve the safety aspects of the car and a polished aluminum driveshaft resides under the floor. Wheels are polished American five-spokes with custom made center cap and a Ford logo in the middle. The car was built and designed by Todd Hair who also did the interior. Paintwork was applied by Scott Davis, the electrical system was furnished by Charlie's Customs and polishing performed by Danny C.

Cecil Whitaker
1941 Willys Coupe
Pendleton, KY USA

A Dennis Taylor '41 Willys body provided the basis for Cecil Whitaker's radical hot rod. Changes were made to the body in that the whole front end was refined to give it a better appearance and the cowl panel changed to be more like a '39 model. The windshield has been moved forward and opened up to fit the proportions of the car better. Giving the body a more refined style is the rounding of the door corners while the chrome on the side has been made out of chrome plated half-round brass. Spies Haecker paint from Dupont was used on the Willys, Azure Candy Blue on the top with straight silver on the bottom. Mercedes headlights show the way at night and Lexus taillights bring up the rear.

The coupe has been outfitted with 22 and 18 inch Intro wheels with 285/35/22 Dunlop Sport 9000 tires on the back and 215/45s on the front. Powerplant is an LS1 Chevy with a six-speed driving to a 3.27:1 four-link located rear end. The front end uses stainless steel Heidts control arms. Four wheel Wilwood disc brakes haul it down from speed and Air-Ride Technologies suspension all the way round insulate the passengers from the vagaries of undulating road surfaces. Specialty power windows separate the passengers from the elements and Vintage Air air conditioning allows them to control the comfort level inside where they relax on dark blue Ultra leather interior trim by James Carter of Bitchin Stitchin. Phipps pedal controls combined with an Ididit steering column and Billet Specialty steering wheel keep the driver in control while performance functions are monitored by Dakota digital instruments.

Mark Anderson
1936 Ford Roadster
FT Dodge, Iowa USA

The Candy Pearl paint that graces the bodywork of Mark Anderson's '36 Ford roadster is the first thing that commands your attention but look closer and you will notice a horizontal bar grille and molded headlights. One piece fenders and running boards add further to the fully integrated appearance as does the three piece solid hood and lack of external door handles. Molded taillights carry the theme through to the rear.

Holding it all off the ground is a set of Billet Specialties wheels with knock-offs. The rears have 245/40/ZR20 Goodrich Comp TA tires while the fronts carry 205/40/17 Comp TAs.

A nine inch Ford rear end is mounted on semi elliptic springs while the front suspension is a Heidts independent system. The roadster also sports four wheel disc brakes. Power comes from an LT-4 Chevy couple to a 4L60E four speed OD transmission from a Corvette.

Inside there's a polished tilt column with Billet Specialties steering wheel, cream leather, a single cluster of gauges and a column shift keeps the floor space uncluttered.

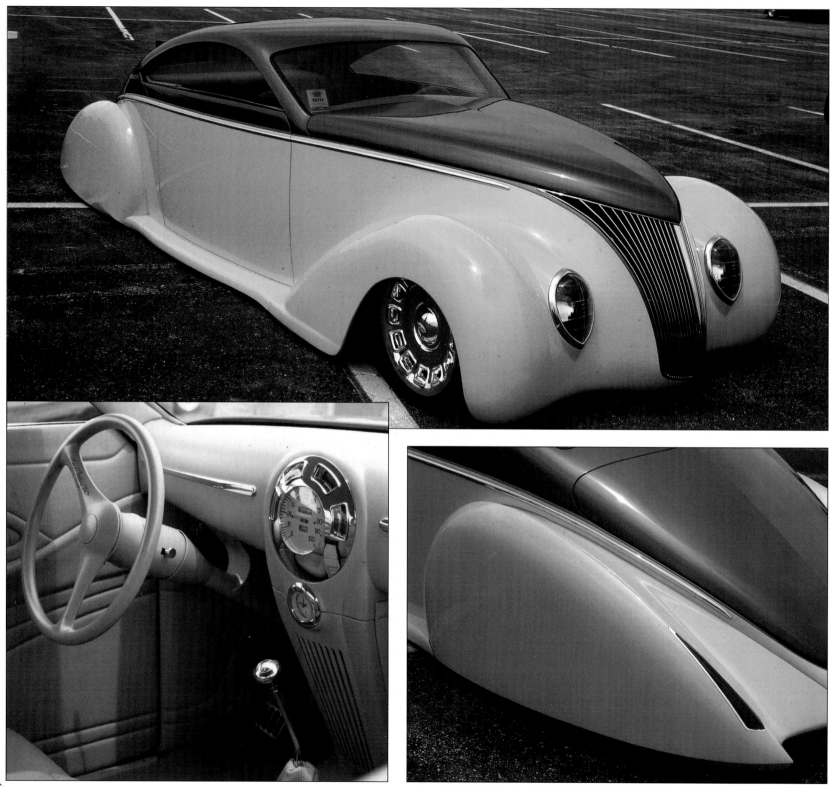

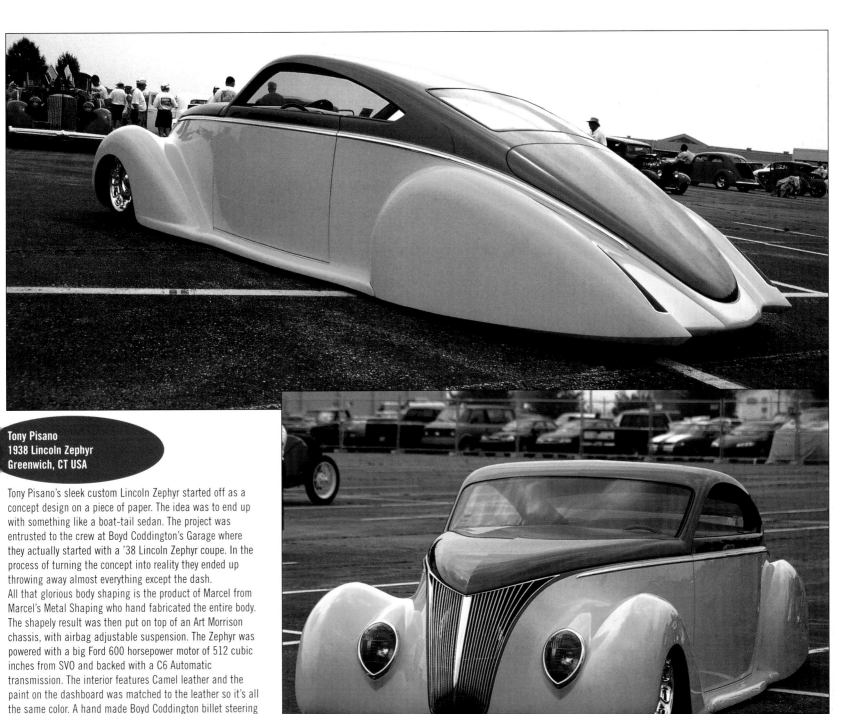

Tony Pisano
1938 Lincoln Zephyr
Greenwich, CT USA

Tony Pisano's sleek custom Lincoln Zephyr started off as a concept design on a piece of paper. The idea was to end up with something like a boat-tail sedan. The project was entrusted to the crew at Boyd Coddington's Garage where they actually started with a '38 Lincoln Zephyr coupe. In the process of turning the concept into reality they ended up throwing away almost everything except the dash.

All that glorious body shaping is the product of Marcel from Marcel's Metal Shaping who hand fabricated the entire body. The shapely result was then put on top of an Art Morrison chassis, with airbag adjustable suspension. The Zephyr was powered with a big Ford 600 horsepower motor of 512 cubic inches from SVO and backed with a C6 Automatic transmission. The interior features Camel leather and the paint on the dashboard was matched to the leather so it's all the same color. A hand made Boyd Coddington billet steering wheel compliments off the interior and a set of 18-inch Boyd Coddington wheels add the finishing touch to the exterior.

You would be hard pressed to pick that Dan Root started with a 1977 MG sports car as a basis for his Ford speedster. Dan cut the MG off at the firewall as he wanted to retain the chrome MG windshield frame that looks more like a Delahaye or Delage. He put a '34 Ford frame underneath the body that straddled the original MG frame extending the wheelbase by 20-inches. Dan was trying to copy the classic '30s French cars as he thought he saw this in regular Ford products. With the '34 Ford frame in place the '34 front fenders were mounted along with '34 running boards. The car was elevated five inches from its standard height which allowed Dan to place a '38 Ford hood and '39 Ford side panels above the '34 fenders. The '39 grille had to be modified to fit as it is normally square at the bottom, but the '34 fenders converge in a V-point. All the teeth were cut off the grille and the bottom half remade to match the V of the fenders. Dan also cut about 15 inches off the grille height because the '38 Ford stood considerably higher. The hood was lengthened 12 inches to reach the MG cowl and reformed along the line where it meets the fenders.

Next Dan cut into the doors exposing the hinges in an effort to get the body to taper into the door. From the seats back all the sheet metal was removed and Dan used '36 Ford rear fenders mated up to the running boards. The '34s are open fenders and the '36 fenders are closed but Dan thought that would make for an interesting combination, again in keeping with a French car from the '30s. Next Dan added a 12 inch extension to the '36 fenders to make them longer and more pointed. The MGB hood was modified and used for the deck lid and the actual MG deck lid went underneath the hood to create the splash apron behind it.

All that remained was to fill in from the MG hood to the fenders with sheet metal to make the sides complete.

The section that goes across behind the back of the seat was cut off the MG and moved forward six inches, elevated an inch and then tilted back to start the slope down to the deck lid. The steel tonneau on the car is removable and that was made from another piece of an MG donor car. A '48 Plymouth steering wheel was adapted to the MG steering column and Dan wound up with a V6 3.4 stroker motor from an S10 Chevy Blazer with T5 five speed aluminum Mustang transmission behind it to motivate the speedster. Fifteen inch wheels have '57 Lincoln hubcaps with different color centers.

Dan bought the rear bumper for $20 from a junkyard and has no idea what it was off. He wanted a clean looking bumper so he just kept it and it worked out fine. He looked for years for a front bumper and ended up using one from a '61 Jaguar 3.8 with the edges cut to match the rear bumper.

Stock MG rear suspension is retained as is the MG rear end. The car may get an eight inch or nine inch Ford rear end underneath it later. The front suspension was also retained as it is designed to carry the aluminum V8 from the factory. However it was cut and widened six inches and fitted with new rubber bushes, new shock absorbers and the MG rack and pinion steering.

The dash is still an MG and Dan bought the simulated wooden stick-on dash material to keep it looking original.

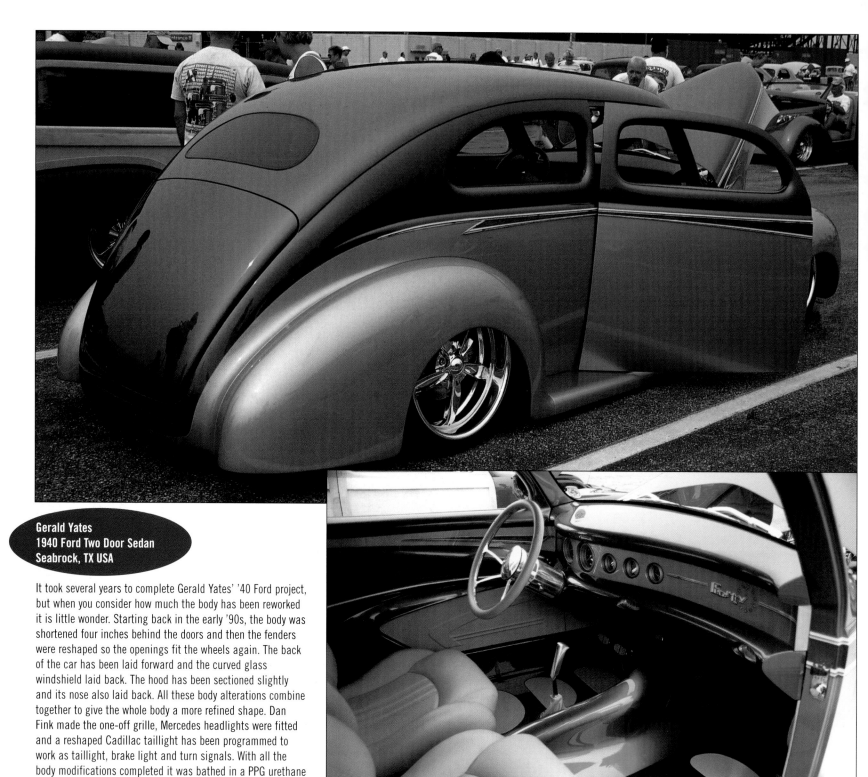

Gerald Yates
1940 Ford Two Door Sedan
Seabrock, TX USA

It took several years to complete Gerald Yates' '40 Ford project, but when you consider how much the body has been reworked it is little wonder. Starting back in the early '90s, the body was shortened four inches behind the doors and then the fenders were reshaped so the openings fit the wheels again. The back of the car has been laid forward and the curved glass windshield laid back. The hood has been sectioned slightly and its nose also laid back. All these body alterations combine together to give the whole body a more refined shape. Dan Fink made the one-off grille, Mercedes headlights were fitted and a reshaped Cadillac taillight has been programmed to work as taillight, brake light and turn signals. With all the body modifications completed it was bathed in a PPG urethane

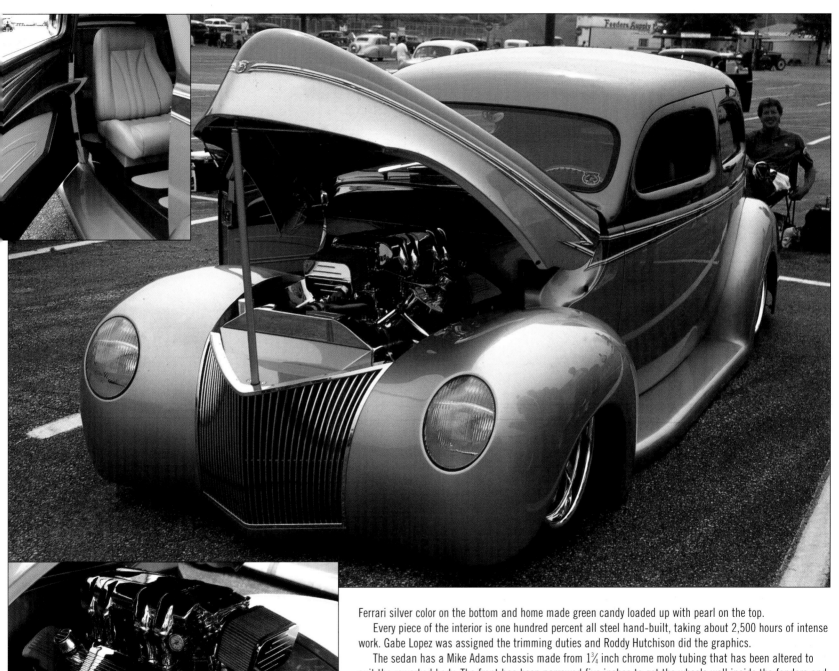

Ferrari silver color on the bottom and home made green candy loaded up with pearl on the top.

Every piece of the interior is one hundred percent all steel hand-built, taking about 2,500 hours of intense work. Gabe Lopez was assigned the trimming duties and Roddy Hutchison did the graphics.

The sedan has a Mike Adams chassis made from $1\frac{3}{4}$ inch chrome moly tubing that has been altered to suit the reworked body. The front has been narrowed five inches to get the wheels well inside the fenders and the overall chassis has been shortened one inch. Slotted between the front rails is a 468 cubic inch big block Ramjet engine backed by a Doug Nash five speed. Suspension is all Corvette with Boyd Coddington wheels, 20 inch diameter on the rear and 17 inch on the front. Tires are Dunlop. Gerald's own shop, Snick's Rod and Custom, did the finished metal work, bodywork, paintwork and the fabrication of the interior.

Larry (Heavy Duty) Frazer
1931 Model A Two Door Tourer
Watertown, TN USA

Starting out with a pair of American Stamping '32 rails Larry Frazer built his own crossmembers and incorporated a Kugel right angle brake master cylinder mechanism to complete the basic chassis. A four-bar system went under the front with a Super Bell axle and VW brakes while the rear also has a four bar system and Wilwood disc brakes. Wheels are American Racing Torq-Thrusts, 15x6 on the front and 17x11 on the rear with BF Goodrich tires.

Powering Larry's Model A is a '57 392 Chrysler Hemi that makes 700 horsepower thanks to a .498" lift cam and six new Holley two barrels on a very rare Weiand intake that feeds a 3% underdriven 6.71 GM blower with three inch drive. Exhaust is handled by a set of home-built zoomies that have been Jet-Hot coated while a Griffin alloy radiator controls engine temperature. A healthy engine needs a strong transmission so Larry went for a built 727 Torqueflite and followed it up with an eight inch Ford truck rear end.

The unique two door Model A uses a Foothills body from North Carolina that came with suicide doors as standard. The red paint is by the owner with flames by Rick Harris. S&H chrome took care of the shiny bits and inside there is a pair of Tea's seats trimmed by Alton Odoum in tan tweed. Larry monitors critical functions via a set of Stewart Warner gauges, gets it rolling thanks to a Lokar shifter and decides which way it will go using an Ididit steering column with Billet Specialties steering wheel.

Mike Cowie called on the skills of Shane Rowe to help bring his '33 hiboy roadster to fruition. The Australian body needed to be fully steeled out so in the process the doors were lengthened to simulate the American equivalent. A rolled rear pan with louvers finished off the back view and a Halibrand Indy filler cap was added to the top of the rear quarter.

The Rod City Repro's chassis was further modified by Southern Rod & Custom to suit the style of the car. The front horns were removed and the panels made to blend the grille into its surrounds smoothly. At the rear the chassis was stepped four inches. Under the front went a Chassis Engineering dropped axle with mono-leaf spring and HQ Holden steering box. Wilwood four spot calipers are used on the disc brakes at both ends of the roadster and they are applied by an XA Falcon master cylinder. The rear end is a Halibrand V8 quick change with 3.55:1 ratio and Pete & Jakes Viper coil-overs. Holding it all off the ground is a set of Real Wheels, 15x4 on the front with 155/15 XZX Michelin tires and 15x10 on the rear with 285/70x15 Goodrich tires.

The engine in Mike's roadster is nothing less than a fully blown 392 Chrysler Hemi, bored .060 inches to

give a final capacity of 408 cubic inches. Filling the gap between the heads is a Cragar blower manifold that mounts a GM 6-71 supercharger with Mooneyham end plates and a custom made drive. Feeding the blower is a pair of 750 Carter carbs. Before it was painted the block was ground smooth and a Weiand big block Chevy water pump adapted. Custom made lakes style headers with four inch megaphones take the exhaust away through a 2-1/2 inch hand made exhaust system. The radiator was made by Aussie Desert Cooler using a Walker tank. The engine was backed with a Race Glide transmission with a Hurst Quarter-Stick shifter.

Special bonnet sides with bubbles to clear the Hemi rocker covers were made up and teamed with the one-piece top with cutout for the blower scoop. Once all the body preparation was completed Shane Rowe applied the PPG Ducatti Yellow paint work and Matt Egan of Extreme Designs applied the superb blended four colour candy flames. Andrew Muirhead was called in to make the seat that was trimmed using scarlet leather by Rod Lingard who also made and covered the lift-off hard top. Red carpet was used on the floor. The filled dash is outfitted with a set of Moon gauges plus a NOS cable drive Stewart Warner tacho and there's a louvered panel tidying up the underside of the dash. SRC made the stainless steel steering column that is topped with a Pete & Jakes Bell style tri-spoke wheel with leather trim.

Finishing off the outside of the roadster is a set of Model A headlights with turn signals hidden inside and a pair of '36 Ford taillights tell following drivers where Mike just disappeared into the night.

Ronald Frederick
1938 Packard Limousine
Gonzales, LA USA

Ronald Frederick purchased his Packard limousine out of Burbank, California but it originally belonged to the William Rigby family (PK Chewing gum) who used it on Catalina Island for ferrying guests from the pier to the family mansion. The Rigby family had two of them custom built just for this purpose. This particular vehicle had always been a stretched limo with 210 inch wheelbase. When found the Packard was in really rough condition and it required a whole new rear clip. Originally built with four passenger doors along the side, Ronald made this into a solid wall and took the center doors out, leaving only one rear door. He also added Dodge wipers and Lambert taillights. Paint is PPG Corvette white base coat/clear coat.

Inside there is a Viper dash, dual air conditioning systems and dual heating. Entertainment is provided by a DVD player and a stereo sound system and the interior is all trimmed in wine colored genuine leather. Of course counter tops incorporating a bar have been built into the interior for the comfort of the guests.

Mechanical upgrades for the Packard included a nine inch rear end from a Versailles and a Chevrolet independent front suspension, all equipped with Air-Ride suspension. The task of hauling the huge Packard around falls to a Dodge V10 engine with six-speed transmission. In driving trim the hefty Packard weighs 6400 pounds and rolls around on Boyd Coddington wheels.

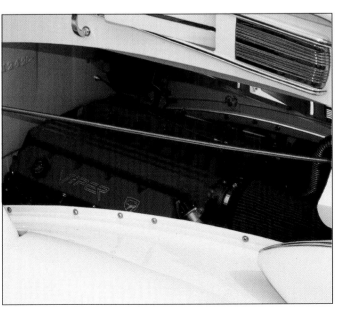

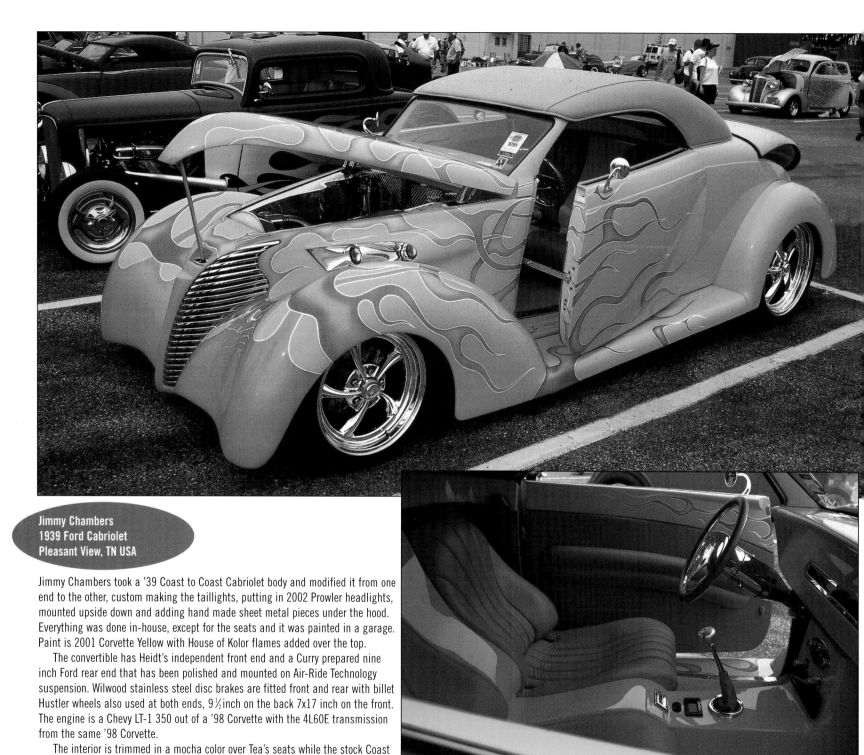

Jimmy Chambers
1939 Ford Cabriolet
Pleasant View, TN USA

Jimmy Chambers took a '39 Coast to Coast Cabriolet body and modified it from one end to the other, custom making the taillights, putting in 2002 Prowler headlights, mounted upside down and adding hand made sheet metal pieces under the hood. Everything was done in-house, except for the seats and it was painted in a garage. Paint is 2001 Corvette Yellow with House of Kolor flames added over the top.

The convertible has Heidt's independent front end and a Curry prepared nine inch Ford rear end that has been polished and mounted on Air-Ride Technology suspension. Wilwood stainless steel disc brakes are fitted front and rear with billet Hustler wheels also used at both ends, 9½ inch on the back 7x17 inch on the front. The engine is a Chevy LT-1 350 out of a '98 Corvette with the 4L60E transmission from the same '98 Corvette.

The interior is trimmed in a mocha color over Tea's seats while the stock Coast to Coast dash has color digital gauges. Ididit supplied the steering column that is topped with a Billet Specialties steering wheel.

Tony Southwick
1941 Willys Coupe
Liberty, MO USA

Tony Southwick's Willys project got under way with the purchase of a five year old Dennis Taylor body from a buddy. Having bought the body Tony then purchased the wheels and tires he wanted and figured out the stance for the car. Then he built the frame to suit. Underneath went Air-Ride suspension and into the engine bay went a 427 Chevy with big .592" lift cam, but small 9:1 pistons to suit running it on the street on pump gas. Feeding the engine is an 800 cfm Edelbrock carburetor. The rear end was tubbed to suit the 12 inch tires, but the car was built to drive and is suitable for running on

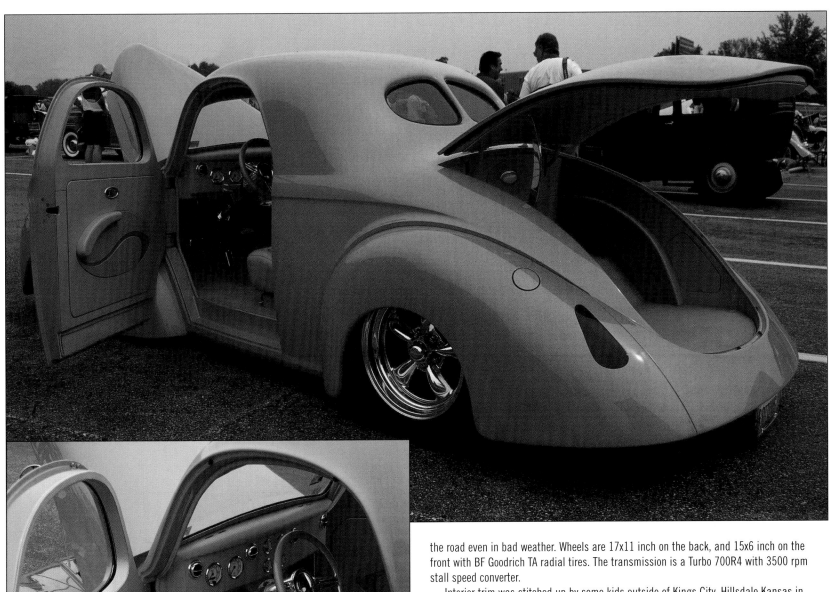

the road even in bad weather. Wheels are 17x11 inch on the back, and 15x6 inch on the front with BF Goodrich TA radial tires. The transmission is a Turbo 700R4 with 3500 rpm stall speed converter.

Interior trim was stitched up by some kids outside of Kings City, Hillsdale Kansas in cream color leather. The hides were sent down to be embossed with the appearance of a baby alligator, they just put a little dye in the color to make it look that way. Tony then added a little birds-eye maple to the interior, just to break it up. The steering column is from Ididit with a custom made three inch longer horn adapter so Tony could drive the car in more comfort. The dash is fitted with VDO Cockpit Royale gauges. Exterior paint color is PPG Tangerine, a Hotlicks color from what they call their Hotlicks Group, usually reserved for Lamborghinis.

John Claydon now lives in Australia but he is a recent arrival from the UK where his radical Willys coupe was originally built at his Intensive Care Custom and Repair Shop and driven on the street.

The body is an original steel version with fiberglass front panels and Kevlar rear wheel arches, all bathed in Purple Candy Apple with Pearl Pink highlights.

A Pro-Mod chassis was constructed from CDS tubing and it incorporates a sealed breather system. The engine is a blown 392 Hemi Chrysler with Hilborn injection and nitrous oxide injection driving to an Art Carr Turbo 400 transmission. A strengthened nine inch rear end fitted with Strange axles and a Detroit Locker centre is located by a four link system with track locater and Spax adjustable coil-overs. Up front we find Leda struts with custom made A-arms. JFZ brake calipers grab the rotors that reside behind 14x15 and 3½x15 Weld Superlite wheels fitted with Mickey Thompson 33x21.5x15 and 26x7.5x15 tires.

John and any passenger game enough sits in Jazz seats with Deist harnesses and there's a window net on the driver's door. Black Wilton carpet lines the floor and the headliner is Rolls Royce material. The Willys also features an electronic fire suppression system.

It took Joe Kovi and Laura Barbiche seven years to build their stunning '33 Willys two door woody. A Willys Unlimited chassis was the basis for the woody with Morrison Air-Ride suspension, a nine inch Ford rear end and Wilwood disc brakes all around. Stuffed in the small engine bay is nothing less than a 502 big block Chevy with alloy heads, Victor Junior tunnel ram manifold and a Turbo 400 automatic transmission. A three inch stainless steel exhaust system takes care of the waste gases and a Griffin alloy radiator keeps engine temperature under control.

Colorado Custom wheels are 18x10 at the rear with BF Goodrich tires and 15x5 on the front, again with BF Goodrich tires. Fiberglass panels used on the wagon are from Willys Unlimited with the windshield laid back to match the angle of the grille. The main structure of the woody body is all maple with accent trim in tiger maple. Keeping it all in pristine condition is five coats of sealer followed by 15 coats of acrylic urethane, the last 10 of them all hand sanded for a perfect finish that is as smooth as glass. Marine waterproof canvas was used to trim the exterior of the roof.

Inside a Buick tilt column with Colorado Custom wheel faces the driver who, along with the passenger, sits on '91 Mazda Miata seats trimmed in fawn leather. Dakota Digital gauges are featured in the dash while the gas tank and air controls are mounted under the van floor. Passengers are kept comfortable by Vintage Air air conditioning, Billet Specialties taillights keep following vehicles informed of the Willys' whereabouts in the dark and the pedals are from Lokar. Door handles and wipers are Juliano's items.

Bob and Karen Schumacher
1933 Ford Cabriolet
Independence, MO USA

A Pete and Jake's bare bones chassis forms the basis of this state of the art '33 Ford roadster. It features hairpin front and rear radius rods with a drilled I beam front axle giving a traditional feel to the car. That's further enhanced by '61 Buick finned brakes on '47 Ford spindles. At the rear there's a popular nine inch Ford rear end with drum brakes but in the engine bay is a not so common 4.6 litre Mark VIII Lincoln engine. Hand-made induction belies the current technology induction system that has three mass airflow sensors although only one is actually functional. Maintaining the deception is a Hilborn scoop. Owner built headers have been HPC coated while a Griffin alloy radiator keeps the operating temperatures where they belong. The automatic transmission is an electronic O/D unit.

The fiberglass reproduction body is a Downs cabriolet painted in PPG Solar Yellow and it features a functional rumble seat and lift-off top for wet days. The interior is trimmed in Pecan Ultra leather, the gauges are Stewart Warner "Wings", and an Ididit column supports a Carriage Works wheel. Norm Grabowski fashioned one of his unique wooden shifters for the roadster that uses Halibrand 15x6 and 15x12 wheels fitted with Kelly 31.5/70 rear tires and Goodyear 195/60 front tires. Steering box is Vega, set up in cross steer fashion, the batwings came from So-Cal and the roadster uses '35 Ford headlights. To keep the style in rhythm from front to back the chassis was lengthened and pinched and it has a '32 style gas tank at the rear.

It's hard to build a street rod in France, because the interest in the hobby is not widespread like it is in the USA or some other European countries. Street rodding survives there thanks to the FSRA and motivated rodders like Frank Gautier.

Frank was for many years a winery specialist and was responsible for a famous "Cote de Baux de Provence", a delicious red wine. After years in the wine industry he opted for a change, and now builds luxury pools in a part of France where high rollers from all over the world have houses. St Remy de Provence is a very quiet and small village, but this old style place is located close to a very popular tourist mountain, the "Baux de Provence". Frank is so proud of his birthplace, we had the chance to shoot his new car in this incredibly scenic area.

The first step into custom cars for Frank was fifteen years ago when he built a Peugeot 203, turquoise with jacked-up rear, that's how it was at that time! After some time away from the hobby, when children came along, Frank was ready to build a new car. The first version of his '34 was powered by a Chevy Monza 305 engine, but the frame was not really efficient with a Volvo 240 rear end, and some minor details needed changing, indicative of the car having been built in a hurry. Frank decided to take his time and turn the project into the ultimate Hot Rod!

He modified the frame for strength, because now the engine is a brand new 350 Chevy, with the TH350 transmission rebuilt. It was repositioned in the '34 frame, now suspended with air bags front and rear and the tank and compressor placed inboard. With 15 centimeter road clearance the car rides comfortably, but the best thing about this suspension is being able to lower the car when parked. The Volvo rear end was swapped for a Jaguar, an old classic maybe, but it is always a good independent system with discs brakes. The steering, front brakes and some other parts came from a Ford Granada.

The body came from an English company '34 Corner, and Frank used French LSA fenders, from a company that's been into rods for twenty years. The engine hood cantilevers to give plenty of access to the engine. Taillights are made from the old Chevy Monza that previously served as a donor car for this rod!

Bernard Geynes who painted the body using a colour from a Peugeot 405 coupe, also made the billet bases for the turn signals that were made by Max Fabre, another old time hot rodder from France. His business is anodizing parts, and he treated the dashboard and all special small billet accessories to that process. Billet Specialties supplied the wheels, steering wheel and other parts to finish off the five year project, and the quality and comfort when driving is fantastic.

acknowledgments

Photographs used in this publication are predominantly from the collection of the author Larry O'Toole with the exception of Pages 74-76 and 34-35 supplied by Anders Oderholm, pages 108-111 supplied by Alain Sauquet, pages 70-71 supplied by Paul Beck.
The author would like to express his gratitude to the owners of all the vehicles featured in this book for their co-operation in supplying the technical information and background stories on their hot rods.

Author Larry O'Toole has been the publisher and editor of Australian Street Rodding Magazine since it began in 1977, a position unique in the hobby of street rodding anywhere in the world. He is also the author of several best selling books on hot rodding including Nostalgia Street Rods, Colorful World of Street Rods, Street Rods in Color, Street Rodding Gallery, The Good Old Aussie Ute, Chopping Tops, Engineering Street Rods and Styling Street Rods.

Susan and Len Finmark from Saugus CA own this yellow '32 Ford hiboy coupe that has a blown 354 Hemi Chrysler engine and rolls on Halibrand wheels.